ABSOLUTELY DELICIOUS!

ABSOLUTELY DELICIOUS!

a collection of my favorite recipes

written and illustrated by

LINDA ALLARD

RANDOM HOUSE
NEW YORK

Library of Congress Cataloging-in-Publication Data

Allard, Linda (Linda Marie).
Absolutely delicious / Linda Allard. — 1st ed.
   p.   cm.
  ISBN 0-679-43305-8
  1. Cookery. I. Title.
  TX714.A446 1994
  641.5—dc20   93-33244

Manufactured in the United States of America
9 8 7 6 5 4 3 2
First Edition

I would like to dedicate this book to my father. He instilled in all of us a love of nature and all things natural, a love of working the land and reaping its harvest, a love of preparing the bounty provided for us.

And to my mother, whose patient and loving instruction taught us how to cook and sew as well as much, much more — and who always set the Sunday dinner table with her best china and silver just for the family.

Above all, both instilled in us a love of family. I remember the happy times.

ACKNOWLEDGMENTS

Thank you to all the people at Random House, especially Jason Epstein, Deborah Aiges and Janis Donnaud, who patiently initiated me into the world of publishing.

A special thank you to Don Ziccardi for seeing the possibilities and then making them happen.

Thank you, Daria Bodner, for your meticulous and unfailing work and the long hours you spent on all the phases of this book — as well as keeping me organized throughout.

A toast to H. G. who came up with the perfect title for the book and for being a good friend for so many years.

Finally, thank you to all my family and friends for sharing all the wonderful food experiences that we have enjoyed together over the years.

PREFACE

Cooking is more than preparing food. Cooking to sustain those you care for, cooking a favorite dish for a favored person, cooking special foods for special occasions — all involve thoughtfulness and love.

Cooking is a sensual experience. Food looks beautiful — vegetables fresh from the garden are as lovely as anything in nature. Food smells good — bread baking and soup simmering are inviting fragrances. Sometimes food even sounds good — sizzling, gurgling and popping all suggest something wonderful is happening in the kitchen. Food feels good — I love the cold, smooth texture of ice cream. Best of all, food tastes good!

Cooking does not have to be grand or complicated to be good. Sometimes the best food is the simplest. Even the most basic food should be prepared well and with care. It should be attractively presented and served at the proper time. Do not let food sit. Toss the salad just before serving. Serve hot food hot.

In Italy there is a phrase, "a tavola," which means "to the table." When that phrase is called out, everyone gathers at the table, and only then is the pasta drained, sauced and served.

The recipes in this book are a collection of my personal favorites. Some are heirlooms passed down from my grandmothers. Some are things my father loved to eat and some are his recipes. Some come from my mother and the way she taught us when we were young. Some are recipes from friends. These are the recipes I use again and again.

I have included exact amounts when that seems important. In many recipes, however, I allow for the cook's personal taste and judgment.

Most of the recipes are uncomplicated, good, country food. I hope you find some favorites.

Contents

Appetizers and Antipasto

APPETIZERS AND ANTIPASTO

I don't like to serve too many or too elaborate appetizers — unless the meal itself is very light — then a large antipasto platter is wonderful — or you can make a whole meal of appetizers!

If you are taking the time to prepare a wonderful meal — you want everyone to have an appetite when you sit down to eat.

An antipasto platter is quick and easy. Arrange slices of prosciutto, salami, pepperoni, and perhaps a bit of cheese. Add a few olives and some roasted pepper slices. Serve with good bread and a glass of wine.

The roasted peppers can be made as described in Grilled Vegetables. Marinated with oil and garlic, they will keep a week or longer in the refrigerator. I usually grill more than I need for a meal so I have them on hand. The marinated mushrooms are also a nice addition to the antipasto platter.

The Artichokes Roman style on page 120 make a delicious first course or – cut into quarters – you can add them to the anti-pasto. Prosciutto, sliced paper thin and arranged on ripe melon slices, is perfect in melon season.

If I want just a tidbit with drinks, before sitting down for the first course, I serve a simple bruschetta or crostini.

BRUSCHETTA

Bruschetta is toasted bread with
garlic and oil — the original garlic bread.

12 slices of good rustic bread — cut ½" thick
1-2 garlic cloves — cut in half
⅓ — ½ cup virgin olive oil

It is essential that the bread is a good rustic loaf — a baguette is preferred. If you use a larger loaf cut the slices in half or in quarters. It is also essential to use a good fruity olive oil.

Toast the bread over hot coals — or in a broiler — until it is golden at the edges and has golden grill marks. It should still be soft inside.

Quickly rub the hot bread with the cut side of the garlic halves — place the slices on a serving platter in a single layer.

Drizzle the olive oil over the bread. You don't need to drown the bread — but drizzle enough so you can taste it. Serve immediately!

This is perfectly simple and perfectly delicious. Serves 4 - 6.

TOMATO AND BASIL TOPPING FOR BRUSCHETTA

1-2 medium tomatoes
1 garlic clove, finely minced
5-10 basil leaves, finely chopped or shredded
a few parsley leaves, finely chopped
1-3 Tablespoons good olive oil
salt and freshly ground black pepper

Pour boiling water over tomatoes and let stand for 30 to 60 seconds. Pour off hot water and replace with cold water. Let tomatoes cool. Peel the tomatoes — the skins should come off easily. Cut tomatoes in half, scoop out the seeds. Place the tomato halves on a paper towel to drain.

Chop the tomatoes into small dice and put in a glass or earthenware bowl. Add garlic, basil, parsley and oil. Season with salt and pepper and toss. Let marinate for 20 to 30 minutes.

Prepare bruschetta as described on page 5.
Top with a spoonful of tomato topping
and serve immediately.
   Topping for 12 - 16 Bruschetta.

Bruschetta With White Beans

1 cup Tuscan beans, recipe on page 153.
12 slices Bruschetta
24 arugula leaves, shredded
24 roasted red pepper slices
virgin olive oil — if desired
freshly ground black pepper

Purée the beans in a food processor until smooth. Prepare peppers as in Grilled Vegetables on page 109. Wash the arugula leaves and remove tough stems. Prepare the Bruschetta on page 5.

Smooth a spoonful of bean purée on the Bruschetta. Top with shredded arugula and roasted red peppers. Grind a bit of black pepper on top and serve immediately.

I keep a jar of red pimentos in the pantry along with a can of cannellini beans — all I need is a loaf of good bread for a quick and easy appetizer. Serves 4 - 6.

CROSTINI

Crostini are smaller than Bruschetta and toasted a slightly different way.

24 slices of a good bread — 1/4" thick slices of a baguette or thin loaf is best
1/4 to 1/3 cup good fruity olive oil
1-2 garlic cloves, cut in half
chopped parsley — if desired for garnish

Brush bread slices on both sides with olive oil. Bake on cookie sheets in a 400° oven until golden — about 5 to 10 minutes. You may want to turn bread over to toast both sides.

Rub slices with garlic halves. Sprinkle with a little chopped parsley, if desired.

Serve immediately or at room temperature.

These are delicious as a topping for soup instead of croutons. Serves - 6 to 8.

Pinzimonio

This is a very simple appetizer. Wash and trim some seasonal vegetables. Celery, carrots, finocchio and radishes are good in the winter. Cucumber sticks and red pepper slices are wonderful in the summer. Any fresh, raw vegetables will work.

Assortment of fresh vegetables, washed and trimmed
½ cup good fruity olive oil
salt and freshly ground black pepper

Cut the vegetables into sticks or wedges —
or leave whole if they are small. I find the
vegetables more attractive if you leave
some small leaves on the radishes, carrots
and celery.
Arrange the vegetables attractively on
a platter.
Pour the olive oil into a small bowl. Add
a bit of coarse salt and freshly ground
black pepper. Mix well.
Place the bowl on the platter with the
vegetables and serve.
This is best served around a table —
as the olive oil does drip a bit — or serve
it in the kitchen while everyone helps
prepare the meal. Serves - 4 to 6.

MARINATED MUSHROOMS

1 – 1 1/2 pounds mushrooms
2/3 cup good olive oil
3 – 4 garlic cloves, sliced
1/4 cup white wine
juice of 1 lemon
2 – 3 sprigs parsley
2 – 3 sprigs thyme
2 – 3 basil leaves
2 bay leaves
10 – 12 peppercorns
salt to taste

Clean the mushrooms. Do not wash mushrooms— the water steals their woodsy flavor and makes them soggy. Use a mushroom brush or a damp paper towel.

I prefer to use whole small mushrooms— but if they are not available slice large mush- rooms into thick slices or cut them in halves and quarters.

In a large skillet - enameled cast iron works best — heat the olive oil over medium heat. Add the garlic slices and cook for a minute. Do not let the garlic brown. Add the mushrooms and toss in the hot oil for a few minutes. The mushrooms will absorb the oil. Add the remaining ingredients and simmer for 3 to 5 minutes.

Pour into a glass or earthenware bowl, cover with plastic wrap and let cool. The mushrooms are best if they marinate for at least a day. They keep well in the refrigerator and are handy to have on hand for part of an anti- pasto platter. Be sure to bring them to room temperature before serving.

Guacamole

2 medium avocados, peeled and pitted
juice of 1/2 lime
1 medium tomato, peeled, seeded and chopped
1 small onion, chopped
1 garlic clove, minced
1 - 2 teaspoons chopped cilantro
1 - 2 jalapeno peppers, seeded and chopped
salt to taste

Mash the avocados with a fork until coarsely chopped. Add the lime juice.

Stir in the remaining ingredients and mix gently.

You may want to add the jalapenos a bit at a time — 2 will be fairly hot — so add until it is fiery enough.

Taste for salt and cilantro.

Pour into a glass or earthenware bowl and serve with corn chips.

If you have made a Pico de Gallo Salsa from page 16 you may add some of the salsa to the mashed avocado and lime.

Do not prepare guacamole too long before your serving time — as it will darken on the top. If you put plastic wrap right on the salsa it will help prevent discoloration.

The darkening will not change the taste — but it does not look very attractive.

Serves 8-10.

Pico de Gallo
Red Salsa

1 small onion, chopped
2-3 medium tomatoes, peeled, seeded and
                                chopped
1-3 jalapeno peppers
1-2 Tablespoons chopped cilantro
1-2 Tablespoons olive oil
salt to taste

Combine all the ingredients in an earthenware bowl — except the oil. You may want to add the jalapenos a bit at a time, until the sauce is spicy enough.

Add enough oil to smooth out the sauce. Taste for salt.

Serve as a dip for corn chips or as a salsa for Mexican dishes. It's a wonderful sauce for grilled fish. This is a fresh sauce that does not keep well. It is best to make it 2 or 3 hours before serving. Serves 6-8 with chips.

Soups

Soups

Soup is a wonderful food. It is heartwarming and homey and very satisfying.

Heavy, hearty soups are terrific meals for lunch or supper. Add a crusty loaf of bread and a salad and top off with dessert. Simple and good.

Soups can also be an elegant first course. I would select the lighter soups or lighten up some of the thicker soups. Add cream to the split pea soup and top with crostini or croutons. Add half-and-half to the potato soup and top with chopped chives.

Soups are easy to make and most freeze well. The soup can be placed in containers and heated quickly for an almost instant meal.

Chicken Broth

1 whole chicken – plus any extra wings
or backs
1 – 2 medium onions, cut in half
2-3 carrots, cut into 2" pieces
1-2 stalks celery, cut into 2" pieces
2-3 sprigs parsley
1/2 teaspoon thyme leaves
1 Tablespoon salt
10 – 12 peppercorns

Put everything in a deep stockpot. Cover with cold water.

Bring to a simmer — don't boil it — keep it at a slow, steady simmer. If any scum rises to the top — skim it off. Cook uncovered until chicken is tender. It should take about 1 hour — a larger or older chicken will take longer. When chicken is tender remove it and let it cool.

Strain the broth and discard the vegetables.

Save the chicken for another use.

If you have the time, chill the broth — the fat will congeal on the top and can be easily removed.

If you are using the broth and don't have time to chill it — skim off the fat and pick up the remaining fat particles with a crumbled paper towel — or skim an ice cube over the surface of the broth to pick up the fat particles.

Freeze the broth if you will not be using it in a few days. It freezes well and if you freeze it in small containers, you will have a cup or two to use whenever a recipe calls for broth.

Makes 1 quart.

Chicken Soup with Noodles

1 chicken and the broth from previous recipe
1 cup egg noodles — I prefer very fine noodles —
    but any size will do

Follow the recipe for chicken broth. After straining and defatting broth, return the broth to the stockpot and simmer — without cover — to reduce the broth to a rich tasting soup.

This usually takes ½ hour or so. Taste and reduce until you think it is rich enough. Taste for salt.

Remove the skin and bones from the chicken and cut into bite-sized pieces.

Add egg noodles and chicken to the reduced broth. Cook until the noodles are tender — about 5-8 minutes for fine noodles. Serve hot.

There is nothing more comforting than a big bowl of chicken soup. Whenever I feel under the weather I get out the stockpot and make this healing soup. Serves 4.

Escarole and Rice Soup

1 medium head escarole
2-3 Tablespoons olive oil
1 medium onion, chopped
3-4 cups chicken broth
1/2 cup rice
freshly grated Parmesan cheese

Clean and trim the escarole. Save the golden heart for a salad. Cut the dark green leaves into 1/2" to 1" ribbons.

In a large, heavy pot sauté the onion in the oil. Cook until the onion is golden. Add the escarole and toss until it is covered with oil and begins to wilt.

Add the chicken broth and rice. Cover and cook until rice is tender.

Serve hot with grated Parmesan cheese on top. Serves 4.

Potato Soup

1-2 medium onions, chopped
2 stalks celery, chopped
3-4 large potatoes, peeled and cubed
Salt and freshly ground black pepper
2-4 cups milk or half-and-half

Put onions, celery and potatoes in a heavy stockpot. Barely cover with water. Add salt.

Bring to a simmer, cover and cook until vegetables are tender, about 15 - 20 minutes.

Add milk or half-and-half — add enough to make the soup as thick or as thin as you like. Cook over medium heat until milk is heated through. Do not boil.

Grind pepper on top and serve hot.

This is my mother's recipe. When we were growing up and were snowbound, we usually had this soup and a peanut butter sandwich for lunch. For a more elegant soup — purée the vegetables, use half-and-half and serve topped with chopped chives. Serves 4 - 6.

Corn Chowder

5–6 slices thick bacon, cut into 1/2" pieces
1–2 onions, chopped
4–5 medium potatoes, diced
1–2 cup corn kernels
2–4 cups milk or half-and-half
salt and freshly ground black pepper

Sauté the diced bacon in a large, heavy soup pot. As the bacon begins to render its fat, add the onion. Continue to cook over medium heat until the onion is wilted — do not brown the bacon — it should just cook through.

Add the potatoes, cover with water and cook until almost tender. Add the corn and continue to cook until the vegetables are tender. Taste for salt.

Add the milk or half-and-half to make soup as thick or thin as you like. Heat through. Do not boil. Season to taste. Grind pepper on top. Serves 6–8.

Split Pea Soup

1 medium onion, chopped
1 medium carrot, chopped
1 stalk celery, chopped
2 medium potatoes, cubed
2 cups yellow or green split peas
salt and peppercorns

Pick over peas and eliminate stones or peas that are not good. Wash and drain them. Put peas along with other vegetables in a large, heavy pot. Cover with water and cook, uncovered, until peas are soft and tender — about 2 hours. As it cooks, you may need to add more water. Stir from time to time to prevent sticking.

Purée in a food processor or pass through a food mill. Taste for seasonings. Return to pot and heat through. Serve hot with crostini or croutons on top.

You may add a piece of bacon or a ham bone at the start. It's delicious with or without. Serves 6-8.

MINESTRONE

26

MINESTRONE

Minestrone means "big soup." It is a hearty vegetable soup that varies from region to region in Italy — based on typical vegetables from each region. My favorite is based on the following ingredients — but any vegetable can be added.

2-3 Tablespoons olive oil
1 clove garlic, cut in half
1 medium onion, chopped
2 medium carrots, diced
1 stalk celery, diced
2 large potatoes, cubed
1-2 cups chopped tomatoes — may be canned
1-2 cups broth or water
1 cup shredded green vegetable — cabbage or
                kale or spinach
1 cup cooked beans, cannellini or other
1/4 to 1/2 cup small pasta — I use tubetti
       or break spaghetti into small pieces
salt and freshly ground black pepper

Sauté the garlic and onions in the olive oil. Use a heavy, large pot. When onion is golden, add the carrots, celery and potatoes, and toss for a few minutes to coat the vegetables with the oil.

Add the tomatoes and broth or water. Bring to a simmer and cook for at least 1 hour. Do not cover. The vegetables should be tender and the soup thick. You may need to add more liquid as the soup cooks. Taste for salt.

When the vegetables are tender add the shredded greens and the cooked beans, and cook for another 15 - 20 minutes.

Add the pasta and cook until the pasta is tender — about 10 minutes. You may need to add more water.

The soup should be very thick and the vegetables soft and mellow.

Serve hot with freshly grated Parmesan cheese. Serves 6-8.

Beef Broth

2-3 pounds beef bones or
    2 pounds of inexpensive stew meat
        in one or two pieces or a shin bone
        with meat on it — or a combination
        of bones and meat
1 medium onion, cut in quarters
1 medium carrot, cut in 2" pieces
some celery leaves
a few sprigs parsley
a few sprigs thyme
salt and 10-12 black peppercorns

Place meat, bones, vegetables and seasonings in a large stockpot. Cover with water. Cook, uncovered, at a slow simmer until beef is very tender — about 2 - 3 hours. Remove beef and bones. Strain broth. If you have time, chill the broth. The fat will congeal on top and you can easily scrape it off.

This is a good basic beef broth. It can be frozen in small containers - to have on hand whenever a recipe calls for beef broth.

29

Vegetable Beef Soup

1 recipe beef broth and beef, previous page
1-2 medium onions, chopped
1-2 stalks celery, chopped
2-3 medium carrots, cut into small pieces
3-4 medium potatoes, cut into small pieces
1 cup green beans, cut into 1" lengths
1 cup corn kernels
1 cup lima beans
6-8 tomatoes, peeled, seeded and chopped —
       or 2-3 cups canned tomatoes
salt and freshly ground black pepper

    Pour the broth into a heavy stockpot. Add the onions, celery, carrots, potatoes and tomatoes. Simmer over low heat until vegetables are tender — about 30-40 minutes.

    Cut the cooked beef into bite-sized pieces. Add the beef pieces, corn and beans and continue to cook — for 20-30 minutes — until all vegetables are tender.

This is best cooked slowly over a very low heat, so all the vegetable flavors can meld.

Taste for seasonings and add freshly ground pepper.

Serve hot with homemade bread and a green salad. Serves 6-8.

PASTA E FAGIOLI
Pasta and Bean Soup

1 medium onion, chopped
2-3 Tablespoons olive oil
4 garlic cloves, minced
3 cups chopped tomatoes – may be canned
10-12 fresh basil leaves
1 chile pepper or a few red pepper flakes
handful of Italian parsley, chopped
5-6 cups cooked beans and their liquid,
                    see page 152
5 cups water
4 ounces pasta – elbows, tubetti or broken
                    spaghetti
salt and freshly ground black pepper

In a large, heavy stockpot sauté onion in olive oil. When onion is golden, add garlic. Cook for a few minutes. Add tomatoes and herbs. Cook until the tomatoes begin to thicken and reduce. Taste for salt.

Add the beans and their cooking liquid. Add the water. Cook over medium heat for 15 to 20 minutes — until the beans begin to break down and the soup begins to thicken. Stir frequently to prevent it from sticking. Taste for seasonings.

When you are ready to serve, add the pasta and cook until pasta is "al dente," about 5-10 minutes depending on type of pasta.

Serve immediately on large soup plates.

Let each guest drizzle some good olive oil on top and grate some Parmesan cheese over.

This is a wonderfully hearty soup. It is halfway between a soup and a pasta and should cook down to a thick soup.

Serves 4-8 depending on appetites.

You may use any cooked beans, although cannellini or red kidney beans or a combination of both are traditional.

My Mother's Bean Soup

2 cups dried white beans — navy or Great Northern
ham bone or ham hock
salt and freshly ground black pepper

Pick over beans and eliminate any stones
or beans that are not good. Rinse and put in a
bowl and cover with water. The water should be
at least 2" above the beans. Let soak overnight
or boil for 5 minutes, cover and let stand for
1 hour.

If soaked overnight — rinse and drain beans
and place in a large, heavy stockpot. Cover with
water. Add ham bone. Bring to a boil — careful,
they boil over very easily. Cover and turn
down to a very low simmer. Cook until beans
are very tender — about 2-3 hours. Remove
ham bone. Taste for salt. Add pepper.

Cut any tidbits of ham from the bone and
add to the soup.

You may need to add water as the beans
are cooking. The soup should be thick.

You may purée some beans in a food processor and add them back to the soup—it will make the soup creamier and smoother.

My mother always served this with chopped onions on top along with freshly baked cornbread. It was our Saturday night special.

The ham bone is not absolutely essential—but it makes the soup smokier and more hearty.

I think my mother sometimes added milk before serving — probably when there was no ham.

Serves 6—8.

Squash Soup

1 – 2 squash – about 1½ – 2 pounds –
      cleaned, peeled and cut into 1" cubes
      butternut or buttercup squash are good
¼ cup butter or oil
1 large onion, sliced
1 quart broth
salt and freshly ground black pepper
a sprinkle of cayenne pepper or
      freshly grated nutmeg

Heat the butter or oil in a heavy stockpot. Add the onion and sauté over medium heat until onion is golden. Add the squash to the onions and pour in the broth. Add salt and freshly ground pepper, a little cayenne pepper or a bit of nutmeg.

Cook at a very low simmer until squash is very tender — about 30 minutes.

Purée in a food processor or put through a food mill. Put soup back into pot and heat through. Taste and correct seasonings.

Serves 4-6.

Zucchini Soup

This is a lovely pale green soup with flecks of darker green. It is a wonderful way to use up some of those overgrown zucchini that seem to hide in the garden.

1 large or 2 medium zucchini
2-3 medium potatoes
1-2 medium onions, chopped
2-3 Tablespoons olive oil
3-4 cups broth or water
at least 1/4 cup basil leaves
salt and freshly ground black pepper

Wash the zucchini, slice lengthwise, scoop out the seeds and cut into 1" cubes. You may only need one zucchini if it is large. There should be about equal amounts of zucchini and potatoes.

Peel the potatoes and cut into 1/2" cubes.

In a heavy stockpot sauté the onion in the olive oil until it is golden. Add the zucchini and the potatoes. Toss them in the oil for a minute or two. Add the broth or the water and bring to a simmer. Cook, uncovered, until the vegetables are tender— about 25 – 30 minutes. Add the basil leaves and simmer a few more minutes. This soup is very good with a strong basil flavor — so don't be stingy.

Put in a food processor and purée. Taste for seasoning.

Return soup to pot and reheat. Serve hot with a basil leaf or two on top.

Serves 4 – 6.

This soup will freeze well.

Lentil Soup

2 cups lentils
2-3 Tablespoons olive oil
1-2 medium onions, chopped
2 cloves garlic, chopped
1-2 medium carrots, chopped
1-2 stalks celery, chopped
2 cups tomatoes, peeled, seeded and chopped
a few sprigs parsley, chopped
a few thyme leaves
salt and freshly ground black pepper

Pick over lentils and rinse. Pour the oil into a heavy stockpot. Over medium heat sauté the onions, garlic, carrots and celery until they soften. Add the tomatoes, lentils and seasonings. Add 8 cups water and cook, covered, at a slow simmer for about 1 hour. The lentils should be soft and beginning to break up. The soup will be thick and chunky. Serve hot with a little Parmesan cheese grated on top. Serves 6-8.

Pasta

PASTA

Pasta is the perfect food. It's good for you — it's low in fat and high in carbohydrates. It comes in so many shapes and sizes and with so many sauces — one never tires of it. It keeps on the shelf — is always on hand to make an impromptu meal. It is quick and easy to prepare. And, best of all, it is delicious!

There are two types of pasta, one made with eggs — The fettuccine and tagliatelle. These are the noodles you can make at home. They are perfect for light and creamy pasta dishes.

The other is the factory-made pasta — spaghetti, maccheroni, linguine, ziti and rigatoni. These are best for hearty, robust sauces.

Pasta should be cooked in lots of water. Four quarts to a pound of pasta is about right. Bring the water to a boil in a large pasta pot. Add the salt, then add the pasta. Do not cover. Bring back to a boil and cook until "al dente." Al dente means "to the tooth" in Italian. It should be cooked through, but still firm when bitten through. Keep testing as pasta is close to "al dente." Do not overcook.

Drain immediately in a large colander. Shake a bit to remove excess water. Pour into a warm pasta bowl. Add the sauce and serve immediately.

"A Tavola."

Tomato Sauce

Pasta with tomato sauce is such a simple combination and so delicious! There are so many ways to make tomato sauce — but I find these simple recipes to be my favorites.

The first is a basic sauce that is good on any type of pasta. It is a good base sauce for other recipes — it is terrific on pizza, see page 197.

The second sauce is made with fresh tomatoes and plenty of fresh basil — best made in the summer when flavorful tomatoes and basil are plentiful.

The third variation is a rich sauce made with butter and tomatoes and wonderful on wide homemade noodles, angel-hair pasta or gnocchi.

The last is an uncooked tomato sauce and can be made only with ripe, fresh tomatoes.

BASIC TOMATO SAUCE

1 clove garlic
1 medium onion, chopped
2-3 Tablespoons olive oil
12-16 very ripe Italian plum tomatoes, peeled, seeded and chopped — or 1 35-ounce can of Italian tomatoes
salt and freshly ground black pepper
6-8 basil leaves

Peel garlic and cut in half. Cook onion and garlic in oil in a heavy skillet over medium heat. When onion is golden add tomatoes, salt to taste and pepper. Cook over medium low heat, uncovered, until sauce thickens and has lost its watery juices — about 20 minutes.

Taste for salt. Add basil and cook for 5 - 10 more minutes.

This will make sauce for about 2 pounds of pasta. It freezes well. I make this sauce in summer when I have lots of tomatoes. It will keep in the refrigerator for a week.

SUGO DI POMODORO

1 clove garlic, sliced or chopped
1/4 cup olive oil
6-8 large, ripe Italian plum tomatoes, peeled, seeded and chopped
1/4 cup chopped or shredded basil
salt and freshly ground black pepper
a few basil leaves for garnish

In a large, heavy skillet sauté the garlic in the oil. Sliced garlic will give a milder flavor, chopped garlic a more intense flavor. Cook over medium high heat until garlic begins to color — do not burn it — burned garlic becomes strong and bitter.

Add the tomatoes and stir well. Season liberally with salt. Lower the heat to medium and cook, uncovered, until the watery liquid has cooked away and the sauce has thickened. This should take about 20 minutes.

When sauce has thickened, remove from heat. Taste for salt. Grind in the pepper. Stir in the basil. Pour over hot pasta and toss well. Garnish with a few basil leaves. Serve at once. This sauce is not served with Parmesan cheese. This will sauce 1 pound of pasta.

A note on preparing tomatoes for these sauces: Fresh tomatoes will peel easily if you drop them into boiling water for 30 seconds and then immediately drop in cold water to cool a bit before peeling. The skins should slip off. Cut tomatoes in half, discard the seeds and coarsely chop the tomatoes.

If you are using canned tomatoes, squeeze the tomatoes over a strainer to remove the seeds but reserve the juice.

Another method is to cut the tomatoes in half and put them in a heavy saucepan. Bring to a simmer over low heat and cook for about 10 minutes or until the skins begin to loosen and slip away. Put the tomatoes through a food mill to remove skin and seeds. This works well with canned tomatoes — you will not need to cook the canned tomatoes before seeding.

In the first method the sauce cooks down to a slightly chunky sauce with bits of tomato. In the second method the sauce is a smooth purée. Either way the sauces are easy and delicious!

TOMATO SAUCE WITH BUTTER AND CHEESE

¼ cup butter
½ recipe for basic tomato sauce, page 45
¼ to ½ cup Parmesan cheese, grated

Melt butter in a heavy skillet over very low heat. When butter has melted add the tomato sauce and simmer a few minutes. Pour hot, drained pasta into the skillet and toss well. Pour into a warm bowl and add the Parmesan cheese. Toss well and serve at once. Pass more Parmesan cheese. Makes sauce for 1 pound pasta.

Pesto

50

Pesto

2-3 cups fresh basil leaves
1-3 cloves garlic
1/4 cup pignoli nuts
1/2 — 3/4 cup good olive oil
1/2 — 3/4 cup freshly grated Parmesan cheese
salt to taste

Wash the basil leaves and spin dry. Put basil, garlic and pignoli nuts into the bowl of a food processor. Mix until a smooth paste forms, scraping the sides of the bowl occasionally. While the processor is running, gradually add enough oil to make a smooth sauce.

Pour into a bowl and add the grated cheese. Mix well. Taste for salt.

Cook the pasta to "al dente" and quickly drain it in a collander—leaving a bit of water on the pasta. Reserve a Tablespoon of pasta water and add it to the pesto sauce. Pour the pesto sauce over the pasta and toss well. Serve at once. Pass more Parmesan cheese.

Pesto is delicious on spaghetti, fettuccine and linguine. I sometimes add a bit of ricotta cheese for a milder, creamier sauce.

This will make more than enough for 1 pound of pasta. Reserve the remaining pesto to add to soups and sauces or use on vegetables. It is delicious on fresh green beans or with green beans and new potatoes.

Pesto is easy to make in the summer when there is plenty of fresh basil. It freezes well.

To freeze or refrigerate — follow the recipe — but do not add the cheese. Spoon the pesto into small jars. Wipe any smears from the inside of the jar with a damp paper towel. Pour olive oil over the top to seal. Make sure all pesto is completely covered with oil.

Put lids on the jars and freeze or refrigerate. As long as the oil covers the pesto it should keep quite well in the refrigerator for several weeks. If frozen, thaw pesto in the refrigerator.

Add the cheese before serving.

Makes 1 to 1½ pints.

PENNE ALL ARRABIATA

1 medium onion, chopped
1 clove garlic, minced
1 - 2 dried chile peppers
3 Tablespoons olive oil
2 - 3 cups tomatoes, peeled, seeded and chopped
salt to taste
1 - 2 Tablespoons chopped parsley
1 pound penne

Sauté the onion, garlic and chiles in the oil in a heavy skillet. Cook until onions and garlic are golden.

Add the tomatoes and salt. Cook over moderately high heat, uncovered, until the sauce thickens. This should take about 20 minutes. Taste for salt and add the chopped parsley.

Cook the penne in boiling salted water until "al dente." Quickly drain and pour into a warm serving bowl.

54

Remove the chiles from the sauce and pour sauce over the pasta. Toss well and serve at once.

The longer the chiles cook in the sauce, the stronger the flavor. Keep tasting the sauce as it cooks down and remove the chiles when it seems spicy enough.

You may use red pepper flakes instead of the whole chiles.

Serves 3 – 4.

BUCATINI ALL AMATRICIANA
Bucatini with Bacon and Tomatoes

5-6 slices thick bacon, cut into ½" strips
1 medium onion, chopped
1-2 Tablespoons olive oil
2 cups Italian tomatoes, peeled, seeded and
                        chopped
1 small dried chile pepper
1 pound bucatini
freshly grated Parmesan cheese

    In a heavy skillet cook the bacon and onion in the oil. Cook over medium heat until the bacon has rendered its fat and the onion is golden.

    Add the tomatoes and the chiles. Add salt to taste.

    Cook over medium heat, uncovered, until the tomato thickens and the fats separate. This should take about 20 minutes. Taste sauce as it cooks — remove the chile when sauce is spicy enough.

56

Cook bucatini in a large pot of boiling water until "al dente." Quickly drain and pour into a warm pasta bowl.

Taste the sauce for salt. Add it to the pasta and toss. Serve immediately. Serves 3—4. Pass the Parmesan cheese.

The chile should add a bit of spice to the sauce, while in Arrabiata it is the center of the sauce.

Both sauces can be used with any sturdy pasta — spaghetti, ziti, penne, rigatoni or bucatini.

The traditional version of Bucatini all'Amatriciana uses pancetta, which is unsmoked Italian bacon. As it is not easy to find — I usually substitute thick sliced bacon.

Penne with Red Peppers

5 – 6 large, sweet red peppers
3 – 4 cloves garlic, cut in half
1/4 cup olive oil
1 – 2 medium tomatoes, peeled, seeded and
                    chopped
salt to taste
20 – 30 basil leaves
1 pound penne
3/4 cup Parmesan cheese

Wash the peppers. With a peeler peel the skins off and discard the seeds. This is a tedious process, but necessary — it is a bit easier if you cut the peppers into thirds or quarters, following the lobes. Cut peppers into ½" strips.

In a heavy skillet sauté the garlic in the oil until it is golden. Cook over medium heat — do not burn the garlic.

Add the peppers and cook over medium heat for 10 minutes. Add the tomatoes and salt to taste. Cook until the peppers are tender and the juice from the tomatoes has thickened. This should take 10 – 15 minutes. Toss and mix the peppers as they cook.

Cook the penne in a large pot of boiling, salted water, until it is "al dente."

Add the basil leaves to the peppers. Leave the basil leaves whole unless they are very large — then carefully tear them in half. Taste for salt.

Quickly drain the pasta and pour into the skillet with the peppers. Toss well. Basil and salt are the only seasonings – be generous with both. Add the Parmesan cheese and toss well. Serve at once.

This is a delicious summer pasta – when basil and peppers are fresh from the garden. You can use red or yellow peppers or a combination of both.
Serves 3 – 4.

This is also delicious served at room temperature as a pasta salad. In this case eliminate the cheese and add a bit more oil. Let the salad marinate for a few hours and then add the basil leaves, toss and serve.

You may also purée this sauce. Cook as above. Add the basil leaves. Put into the bowl of a food processor and purée. Pour over "al dente" pasta and serve. Garnish with a few basil leaves.

For a spicy version of this sauce—you can add a few chile peppers along with the sweet peppers and cook as above. Remove the chile peppers before serving or when sauce is spicy enough. If you purée the sauce, remove the peppers before processing unless you want a really fiery sauce.

The puréed sauce freezes well. Pour into freezer containers, cover and freeze.

Baked Rigatoni

1 recipe basic tomato sauce on page 45
5—6 sweet or hot Italian sausage links —
about 1 pound
1 pound rigatoni
1/2 pound mozzarella cheese, cubed
1 cup ricotta cheese
1/2 cup freshly grated Parmesan cheese

Prepare tomato sauce.
Cut sausage into 1" pieces. In a small skillet cook sausage with 1/4" water. Cook until water evaporates and sausage is browned, about 15 – 20 minutes.
Bring a large pot of water to boil. Add salt and rigatoni. Cook until pasta begins to lose its crisp texture — about 10 minutes. Do not overcook — the pasta will continue to cook while it bakes.
Quickly drain the pasta and return it to the pot. Add the tomato sauce and

sausages and mix well. Add mozzarella and ricotta and toss quickly. Transfer to an oiled, ovenproof casserole — about 1½ quarts. Do this quickly — you don't want the mozzarella to begin to melt.

Top the casserole with the grated Parmesan cheese. If you select a shallow baking dish you will have a lot of crusty cheese on top.

Bake at 350° for about 45 minutes. The cheese should be bubbling and the top crusty and browned.

This is a simple, hearty one-dish meal. Serve with a crusty loaf of bread and a fresh green salad. Serves 4–6.

SPAGHETTI AGLIO E OLIO
Spaghetti with Oil and Garlic

This is one of the easiest of pastas and also one of the tastiest! If you love garlic — this is a winner! Everything you need for this is usually in the pantry — so when I haven't anything fresh to cook, or I come home late, this makes a quick dinner.

Also good for a late night supper — especially after a night on the town — this supposedly helps prevent hangovers!

For two servings:

2/3 pound spaghetti
1/2 cup olive oil
2-4 cloves garlic or more — up to a
        dozen — cut in half or sliced
1/2 chile pepper — more if you like it hot
3 - 6 sprigs parsley, chopped
salt and freshly ground black pepper

Put the pasta on to boil and cook till "al dente." While the pasta is cooking, prepare the oil.

Heat the oil in a heavy skillet. Add the garlic. Sauté over medium heat only until garlic is golden. Do not burn, as burned garlic gives a bitter taste to the oil. Add the chile pepper and the parsley. If the garlic begins to brown, remove it.

When pasta is "al dente," drain it and pour it into a large, warm pasta bowl. Pour the oil over and toss well. Taste for salt. Serve immediately. Pass the pepper mill — but not the Parmesan cheese.

A variation is to add the juice of half a lemon along with the parsley. This adds a piquant touch.

You can use as much or as little of the garlic or hot pepper as you want. Suit your taste — experiment.

You may use red pepper flakes if you do not have dried chile peppers.

Salsa Cruda

This is an uncooked tomato sauce. The combination of hot pasta and the fresh, cool, ripe taste of tomatoes, basil and garlic is fabulous. Do not serve cheese with this sauce.

3-4 large, ripe eating tomatoes
1/2 cup shredded basil leaves
1 clove garlic, minced
1/2 cup good olive oil
salt and freshly ground black pepper
1 pound spaghetti

Peel, seed and chop tomatoes. Place them in a glass or earthenware bowl. Add basil, garlic and oil. Add salt and pepper to taste. Mix and set aside for at least 1 hour.

Bring a large pot of water to boil. Add pasta and 1 Tablespoon salt. Cook to "al dente." Drain and pour into a pasta bowl. Pour sauce over, toss and serve immediately. This is a marvelous summer meal—quick and easy—and delicious! Serves 4.

FETTUCCINE ALLA PANNA
Fettuccine with Cream Sauce

½ pound fettuccine or egg noodles
½ cup butter
½ cup heavy cream
¾ – 1 cup grated Parmesan cheese
freshly grated nutmeg
salt and freshly ground black pepper

Bring a large pot of water to boil. Add fettuccine and 1 Tablespoon salt.

In a large, heavy enameled pan melt the butter over low heat.

When fettuccine is "al dente," drain it and pour it into the melted butter. Toss to coat the fettuccine. Simmer over medium heat and add the cream and cook until sauce is creamy — about 2 minutes. Add the cheese and nutmeg. Toss. Taste for salt and add the pepper. Serve immediately. Pass more Parmesan cheese. Serves 3.

Meats, Fish and Main Dishes

MEATS, FISH AND MAIN DISHES

I like simple grilled and roasted meats and fish — or hearty, robust stews.

Serve a simple pasta or soup before grilled meats or fish, and a vegetable, potato or beans along with the main course. Roasted potatoes, page 148, are good with roasted meats. Tuscan beans, page 153, are traditional with grilled steaks and are also tasty with roast lamb or pork. New potatoes with parsley, page 147, are wonderful with fish. Crispy fried potatoes, page 150, are a natural with fried fish.

With stews I would serve something light first and follow with a green salad. Be sure to have some good crusty bread to soak up the sauce!

Roast Chicken with Rosemary

1 small chicken — about 3 pounds
salt and freshly ground black pepper
2-3 cloves garlic, cut in half
2-4 sprigs rosemary and 1 teaspoon
        chopped rosemary or 1-2
        teaspoons dried rosemary

Wash and clean the chicken well. Pat dry with paper towels.

In a small bowl mix the salt and a generous amount of freshly ground black pepper. Season the interior well with the mixture. Add the garlic and the rosemary sprigs to the cavity.

Sprinkle the mixture of salt and pepper over the exterior. Sprinkle or pat the chopped rosemary on the chicken.

Place the chicken on a roasting rack, breast down, and place the rack in a roasting pan. Cook in a hot oven— 400°—425° for 30 minutes. As the juices begin to flow, baste the chicken. Turn breast side up and continue to roast until chicken is tender and crispy and brown. This should take about one hour.

You may roast potatoes and onions along with the chicken. Cut the vegetables into 2" to 3" pieces — or in quarters or halves. Add to the roasting pan

when you start the chicken. Sprinkle
with salt and freshly ground black
pepper. Add a few garlic cloves and a
few sprigs of rosemary.

As the chicken roasts, toss the
vegetables to coat them with the
drippings.

MARILYN'S ROAST LAMB

1 small leg of lamb — about 5 pounds
5-6 cloves garlic
4-6 rosemary sprigs or 2 Tablespoons
          rosemary leaves
1/2 teaspoon salt
optional:
          6-8 medium potatoes, peeled and
          cut into 2" pieces

Chop the garlic, rosemary leaves and salt in a small food processor or on a cutting board. Place in a small bowl and add 1-2 Tablespoons olive oil — add enough to make a thick paste.

With a small knife cut small slashes in the lamb and stuff the slashes with the paste. Use the end of a chopstick to force paste into the slashes.

Cut a garlic clove in half and rub the lamb with the cut side. Rub the lamb with the olive oil and sprinkle with salt.

Place the lamb in a roasting pan and put it in a hot oven — 425° — for 15 minutes. Turn down to 375° and continue to roast until lamb is cooked to desired state. If you like your lamb pink — allow 20 minutes per pound. If you prefer medium to well done allow 30 minutes or more per pound. Baste every 20 minutes with pan drippings.

Remove from oven and let rest in a warm place for 15 minutes. Carve and serve.

If you plan to add potatoes, add them 1½ hours before you estimate the lamb will be done. Add a sprig or two of rosemary and a few more garlic cloves. Turn the potatoes as the lamb roasts.

A few years ago my brother, David — the architect of my beautiful home — and his wife, Gloria, and I were all visiting Italy to research Palladian villas. My friend Marilyn served this traditional Italian feast for Easter. It was a memorable meal!

ARISTA
Florentine Roast Pork

a pork roast — about 5 - 6 pounds of
loin of pork
2 - 3 Tablespoons oil
a bit of flour
salt and freshly ground black pepper
Basting sauce:
  1/2 cup chicken broth, page 19
  1/2 cup white wine
  1 - 2 cloves garlic, chopped
  1/2 - 1 teaspoon rosemary leaves
  1/4 - 1/2 teaspoon fennel seeds
  1/4 teaspoon nutmeg or a few grindings
    of fresh nutmeg

Rub the roast with the oil. Rub salt,
pepper and a little flour on the roast.
    Put 2 Tablespoons oil into a large, heavy
skillet. Brown the roast over medium high
heat until all sides are browned.

Place the meat in a roasting pan and roast at 350°. Allow about 1/2 hour per pound. Cook to 185° on a meat thermometer.

To make basting liquid, combine the ingredients in a small saucepan. Cook over low heat for a few minutes.

Baste the roast frequently with the liquid and the pan juices. When roast is done remove it from the oven to a warm place and let rest for 15 minutes. Carve and serve.

Serves 6-8.

This is our traditional New Year's Eve roast. It is so good! Last year we roasted it over the fire — it was outstanding!

If roasting over a fire, put the meat on a spit and place over hot coals. Place a heavy iron skillet under the roast to collect the drippings. Keep turning the roast as it cooks and baste as above. Keep the fire hot and keep moving fresh coals under the meat. The cooking time will vary depending on the heat of the coals.

CHICKEN WITH WINTER VEGETABLES

4 whole chicken breasts, skin removed
12 whole small carrots, peeled
3-4 medium parsnips, peeled and halved
2-3 large potatoes, peeled and quartered
16-20 Brussels sprouts, cleaned
1 stalk celery, sliced
5-6 scallions, sliced — use some of the
                    green part
2 Tablespoons chopped parsley
3 cups chicken broth, page 19
salt and freshly ground black pepper

Arrange all ingredients in a heavy skillet or shallow pan with a cover. Pour the broth over the chicken and the vegetables. Season with salt and pepper.

Cook, covered, over medium heat until the chicken is cooked through and the vegetables are tender — about 20 to 25 minutes. Serve in deep plates or shallow soup plates. Serves 4.

Veal Stew

2-3 Tablespoons olive oil
2 pounds rump roast of veal or stewing
      veal cut into 1½" cubes, fat and
      gristle removed
1 medium onion, chopped
1½ cups tomatoes, peeled, seeded and
                  chopped
salt and freshly ground black pepper
2 cups peas, fresh or frozen
3-4 medium potatoes, optional

    Heat oil in a large, heavy skillet. Brown the veal pieces on all sides. Brown only as many pieces as will fit in one layer easily at one time. Remove veal to a flameproof casserole with a lid — about 2½ quarts.
    Add onions to the skillet and cook until golden. Scrape and loosen any of the browned bits and mix with the onions. Add the tomatoes to the onions and cook for a minute or so.

Add the tomato and onions to the meat in the casserole. Season with salt and pepper. Cook over medium heat until the stew begins to simmer. Cover and place in a hot 350° oven. Cook until veal is tender, about 1½ to 2 hours. Taste for seasonings.

When veal is tender add the peas. You may use frozen peas if fresh are not available. Fresh peas will cook in about 10 minutes — frozen peas will only take 5 minutes. Cook only until peas are bright green and are tender.

Serve with a crusty bread to soak up the sauce. Follow with a green salad.

Serves 4 – 6.

If using potatoes — add them about 45 minutes before meat is tender.

This is a wonderful dish to prepare in advance — refrigerate, bring to room temperature, then heat through. Add the peas after reheating. Do not add potatoes if you plan to refrigerate — the texture of potatoes is spoiled in the refrigerator.

Beef Stew with Biscuit Crust

1½ pounds stewing beef, cut into 1½" cubes
¼ cup flour
3 – 4 Tablespoons oil
3 medium onions, chopped
1 stalk celery, chopped
2 cups tomatoes, peeled, seeded and chopped
salt and freshly ground black pepper
4 – 5 medium potatoes, cut into 1½" pieces
3 - 4 carrots, cut into 1½" pieces
biscuit dough recipe on page 186
1½ cups peas, fresh or 1 package frozen peas

Select a 3 quart casserole that will hold all the ingredients and leave a 1" space on top for the biscuit dough.

Dredge the stew meat in the flour. Add the oil to a large heavy skillet. Brown the meat on all sides over medium high heat. Do not crowd. Brown in two batches if necessary. Remove meat and place in the casserole.

82

Add the onion and celery to the skillet and cook until golden. Scrape any browned bits loose and mix in. Add the tomatoes and cook for a few minutes. Pour the vegetable mixture into the casserole. Season with salt and pepper. Cover the casserole and place in a hot 350° oven.

Cook until the meat is almost tender—about 1½ to 2 hours. Add the potatoes and cook until meat and vegetables are tender.

You may need to add broth or water as the stew cooks. The liquid should form a thickened gravy.

Prepare the biscuit dough. Roll out into a shape that will fit the top of the casserole. Cut one or two holes to let steam escape — use a small biscuit cutter or a small glass.

Add peas to the stew and mix in.

Cover the stew with the biscuit dough. It should fill the top of the casserole. Bake at 400° until biscuit crust is golden brown, about 15 minutes. Serve at once. Serves 6.

Braised Lamb Shanks

2–3 Tablespoons olive oil
4 lamb shanks, with bone in – about 1 pound each
2 cloves garlic, cut in half
2–3 rosemary sprigs
3/4 cup red wine
1/4 cup oil-cured black olives
salt and freshly ground black pepper

Heat the oil in a heavy, flameproof casserole that can accommodate all the lamb shanks — about 2 1/2 to 3 quarts. Add the lamb and brown on all sides. Add the garlic, rosemary, red wine and olives. Season with salt and pepper — the olives are salty, so be cautious with the salt.

Cover and turn heat down to a low simmer. Cook until the shanks are tender— about 1 1/2 to 2 hours. Check to be sure there is enough liquid as the shanks cook. Add water if needed.

Place shanks on a serving platter. Pour sauce over and remove rosemary sprigs. Serve at once. Serves 4.

This is a hearty dish. Follow with a refreshing salad — perhaps the fennel salad on page 168.

MOTHER'S FISH BATTER

1 cold egg
1/2 cup ice water
3/4 cup self-rising flour
peanut oil
1 1/2 – 2 pounds fish filets

Break the egg into a bowl. Add the ice water and then the flour. Stir, but leave a bit lumpy. Do not overmix.

You must keep the fish and the batter cold and the oil hot. The difference in the temperature will prevent the oil from penetrating the batter. The fish will steam and the batter will puff and form a golden brown crust.

Heat the oil in a large, heavy skillet to 400°. There should be at least 1/2" of oil.

Dip the fish in the batter and carefully drop them in the hot oil. Fry until brown on one side, turn and brown the other side. Remove and drain on paper towels.

FATHER'S SHORE-FRIED FISH

When you fished with my father, lunch was a shoreside event. If you caught fish in the morning, you had fish fried this way. Pan fried potatoes, coleslaw and Mother's pickles were the usual accompaniments.

If you didn't catch fish, you had potatoes and coleslaw — without the fish.

bacon drippings — about 3-4 Tablespoons
1/3 cup cornmeal
1 1/2 to 2 pounds fish filets

Over hot coals, heat the bacon drippings in a heavy cast iron skillet.

Dip the fish filets in the cornmeal and fry quickly in the hot skillet. It will take just a few minutes on each side. The fish should be golden brown. Serve at once. Serves 4.

Roasted Striped Bass

1 whole striped bass, about 2 - 2½ pounds,
     cleaned and scaled
2 - 3 basil sprigs
2 - 3 rosemary sprigs
2 - 3 parsley sprigs
1 garlic clove, sliced
juice of 1 lemon
salt and freshly ground black pepper

¼ cup white wine
½ cup olive oil
lemon slices and a few basil leaves for garnish

Have the fish market clean and scale the fish, but leave it whole.

Wash the fish and pat dry. Salt and pepper the cavity. Stuff the cavity with the herbs and the garlic.

Select a heavy, shallow baking dish — an enameled cast iron one works well. Oil the pan.

Place the stuffed fish in the pan. Season with salt and pepper. Pour the lemon juice and the wine over the fish. Pour the olive oil over the fish.

Roast the fish in a hot oven at 350° until the fish is tender and flakey. This should take 30 to 40 minutes. Baste the fish several times while it roasts.

Remove the fish to a serving platter. Garnish with lemon slices and basil leaves. If you feel uncomfortable serving the whole fish at the table, remove the skin and carefully remove the fish from the bones and arrange on warm plates. Garnish and serve.

Pour the pan juices into a small pitcher and let your guests pour them over the fish.

You can also make additional sauce by chopping a few basil leaves with a bit of garlic. Mix with the juice of a lemon and some good fruity olive oil and stir.

Any fish can be roasted this way — snapper and salmon are good. You may vary the herbs to suit the fish.

You may also wrap the fish and oil in an aluminum foil packet and place the packet in the roasting pan. The juices will steam the fish and the herbal fragrance is wonderful when the packet is opened. The cooking time will be less than the roasted method — about 20 to 25 minutes. Serves 4.

Cooking over the Fire

COOKING OVER THE FIRE

When we were growing up we did a lot of cooking over the fire. We cooked elaborate meals — potatoes in foil, corn cooked on the coals and various meats. We cooked simple ones — hot dogs and s'mores, those wonderful sticky treats made with toasted marshmallows and a piece of a chocolate bar sandwiched between two graham crackers.

We used to take an annual day trip to a beach on Lake Erie. We would pack up and leave early in the morning. When we arrived we unpacked, had a quick swim and then cooked a great breakfast on the charcoal grills.

That breakfast has developed over the years into the typical Allard camp breakfast. Home-fried potatoes, crisp bacon, scrambled eggs, toast and sweet rolls — along with camp coffee, juice and fruit.

After this hearty meal, we were fortified

to play in the sand and jump in the waves until the sun started to set.

Then we prepared another grand meal— usually picnic fare and something cooked on the grill. At dark all the sleepy, sun-burned kids were packed in the car for the long ride home.

I love the taste of food cooked over the fire. I love the sounds and smells of the food sizzling and sputtering as it grills. I also love the idea that when you grill, you have no pots and pans to clean up.

I like to start with bruschetta when the coals first get hot — that gives you and your guests something to nibble on while the rest of the meal cooks.

I love a whole meal made of grilled vegetables, followed by a salad. But I also love a good steak.

Now that I have my big kitchen fireplace — I cook over the fire year round.

I have a wonderful antique iron grill

with legs that sits on the hearth in front of the fire. The two back legs are longer than the front ones so the grill tilts to the front. As the food grills the drippings run down the grill and are collected in a clever little drip-pan that hooks to the front of the grill.

Any grill will work. Find a few bricks, stack them to the desired height and balance the grill securely on top of them. Scrape hot coals under the grill.

I also cook roasts by suspending them from a crane over the fire. Chicken with rosemary and Florentine pork are delicious cooked this way. And what could be better on a cold wintry day than a pot of beans simmering over the fire?

Grilled Fish

Salmon and swordfish steaks are my favorites for grilling.

You may marinate the fish if you wish. The marinade on page 97 will work well.

Prepare the fire until the coals are hot. You may want to oil the grill before cooking, as fish sometimes sticks.

Put the fish on the grill, cook one side, and turn and finish grilling.

Fish will take about 8 to 10 minutes to cook through for every 1 inch of thickness.

Swordfish on Skewers

1 – 2 swordfish steaks, 1" thick – allow
about 1/3 to 1/2 pound per person
marinade for fish, see recipe on following
page 97
bay leaves – 4 to 6 for each skewer

    Cut the swordfish into 1" cubes.
Marinate fish in a shallow bowl, mixing
to coat all sides, for at least 1/2 to
1 hour.
    On skewers alternate cubes of fish
with bay leaves.
    Grill over hot coals until fish is just
cooked through – about 10 to 12 minutes.

MARINADE FOR FISH

juice of 2 lemons or limes
1/4 cup olive oil
1 - 2 cloves garlic, sliced
salt and freshly ground black pepper
4 - 5 bay leaves

Put all ingredients in a large shallow bowl and mix. Add the fish.

Marinate the fish for at least 1/2 hour, turning to coat all sides.

Grill over hot coals — just long enough to cook fish through — allow 8 to 10 minutes per 1" thickness of fish.

This marinade works well on most fish appropriate for grilling, and is very good for shrimp. Just marinate shrimp and put on skewers and grill.

Makes enough marinade for 1 1/2 to 2 pounds of fish.

Grilled Steak

Steak is the quintessential grilled food. The secret to a delicious, juicy steak with a crusty exterior is to have a red-hot coal bed — to sear the steak over the hot coals and continue to cook it through as the coals cool down.

1 sirloin steak — 1½" to 2" thick

Trim off most of the fat around the edge of the steak. Bring the steak to room temperature.

Prepare the fire until the coals are red-hot. Place steak on hot grill and sear on one side for a few minutes. Turn and sear the other side. Continue to cook on the second side for 5-10 minutes — depending on thickness of steak.

Turn steak back to the first side and continue to grill until meat is cooked as desired.

98

I think steak is best eaten while still red in the center and crusty on the exterior.

Remove steak to a cutting board. Slice and serve immediately. Pass the salt and the pepper mill.

A 2" thick sirloin will serve 6 to 8 — depending on their appetites.

You can judge the progress of the meat by pressing a finger on it. If it is soft to the touch it is still rare to medium-rare. If it is springy, it is medium. If it is firm the meat is well-done. If you are unsure you can always cut a slash in the meat and take a peek.

If the meat has cooked to desired degree and is not properly browned, lower the grill over the coals to brown. You can also move the coals closer together to increase the heat.

Grilled Chops

Follow the instructions for grilled steak on the previous page. The method for grilling chops is the same — the cooking time will vary depending on the size and the thickness of the chops.

1 loin or rib veal chop per person
    or
1 – 2 loin or rib lamb chops per person
optional:
    1 – 2 cloves garlic, cut in half
    rosemary or sage leaves

Have the butcher cut the chops as thick as possible — 1" thick is minimum, 1¼" to 1½" thick is best.

Trim the chops of most of the fat around the edges — leave enough to give flavor to the meat, but remove enough to keep the fat dripping on the fire to a minimum.

If you like garlic and herb flavor — rub the chops with the cut side of the garlic clove and then rub with the herbs. Rosemary is good on lamb and veal. Sage is good with veal.

When coals are red-hot put chops on hot grill. Thick chops will take 5 – 8 minutes per side for medium-rare — depending on size and heat of the coals. Allow more time for well done. Follow the notes for steak to gauge the progress of the chops.

If you can capture the drippings, a lovely sauce can be made with balsamic vinegar.

Arrange the grill at a slight angle — position a drip pan at the low end to catch the drippings as the chops cook.

When chops are cooked remove to a warm platter. Pour drippings into a small saucepan and add 1/2 to 3/4 cup balsamic vinegar. Cook over high heat until sauce is reduced. Pour over chops. Serve at once.

SPIEDINI
Skewered Grilled Meats

for each serving:
  6–7 cubes good rustic bread, about 1½"
  6–7 cubes meat, about 1½"
  1 skewer
  rosemary sprigs or sage leaves
  olive oil

Alternate bread cubes and meat cubes on the skewer — adding either rosemary sprigs or sage leaves here and there as you fill the skewer.

Brush with olive oil and grill over medium-hot coals.

Lamb or veal are delicious. You may also use sausage links that have been cut into 1" lengths.

You can use chicken breasts, cut into 1¼" pieces. The chicken may be wrapped in small slices of prosciutto.

You can make a mixed grill by alternating sausage, veal, chicken and lamb with bread and herbs.

The meat is cut into small pieces so they will cook quickly. The fire should not be as hot as for steaks and chops. Cook until bread is golden brown and crispy and meat has cooked to desired degree. Allow 10 to 15 minutes total cooking time depending on type of meat used and the heat of the coals. Chicken will cook quickly, about 6-10 minutes —until springy to the touch. Veal and lamb will take 10 minutes or so for medium — a little less for rare and more for well done. Sausage should be cooked through — about 15 minutes.

Chicken with Thyme, Mustard and Garlic

1 chicken, cut up
2 Tablespoons Dijon mustard
1-2 cloves garlic
1 teaspoon thyme leaves
1/3 to 1/2 cup olive oil
salt and freshly ground black pepper

Cut the chicken into small pieces.
The breast should be cut in half and the
legs cut into thighs and drumsticks. Wash
the chicken well and pat dry. Put into
a bowl.

Mix the remaining ingredients for the
marinade and pour over the chicken. Toss
to coat all the pieces. Let stand for at
least 1/2 hour.

Cook over medium-hot coals — chicken
is cooked best over long, slow fire. I
usually figure about 1 to 1 1/4 hours.

Place the chicken on the hot grill with

skin side down, brush with marinade. When skin is brown and crusty, turn and brown the other side.

If the coals are too hot the chicken will burn, the drippings will flame up and smoke the chicken — it will be blackened on the outside and not cooked through.

When I'm cooking over charcoal — especially if I'm grilling more than one chicken — I sometimes prepare a second batch of coals so there will be enough hot coals to finish cooking the chicken.

If your grill is large enough add a second group of charcoal to one side of the grill. Move some of the hot coals to the fresh charcoal with fire tongs. The fresh coals should be hot as the original ones lose their heat. Move the hot coals under the chicken and continue to cook.

Sometimes I cook chicken over coals without any marinade or seasoning. The flavor of the charcoal seasons it very well.

Grilled Turkey Breast
over Salad Greens

marinade:
  1/2 – 3/4 teaspoon salt
  1/2 – 3/4 teaspoon dry mustard
  1 clove garlic, cut in half
  3/4 cup olive oil
  juice of 1 lemon
  2-3 Tablespoons Dijon mustard
  freshly ground black pepper

3-4 bunches arugula or 2-3 small heads
      frisée or a combination of salad greens
3-4 slices turkey breast, about 1/2" thick

    Put the salt and dry mustard in a bowl. Mash the garlic halves with a fork into the salt and mustard to release the essence of the garlic. Add the remaining ingredients for the marinade and mix well.
    Pour half the marinade into a shallow bowl and add the turkey slices. Turn to

Coat both sides of the turkey with the marinade. Marinate for 1/2 to 1 hour.

Clean and spin dry the salad greens. Dark and slightly tangy greens are best. A mesclun mix would also be good. See the salad section.

Prepare the grill and get the coals hot. Place the turkey on a hot grill and cook quickly. Turn once to grill the second side and remove to cutting board.

Cut the turkey breasts into 1" wide slices.

Toss the salad greens with the reserved marinade and arrange on 4 plates. Arrange the turkey slices on top and serve immediately.

This makes a quick and easy lunch or late supper. With a crusty bread or a focaccia grilled along with the turkey, it's a delicious dish.
Serves 4.

GRILLED VEGETABLES

108

GRILLED VEGETABLES

2 large red or sweet white onions
4 large red or yellow peppers
2-3 small Italian eggplants
2-3 small zucchini
15-20 large mushrooms
olive oil for drizzling on vegetables
1/4 cup olive oil
1-2 cloves garlic, sliced
salt and freshly ground black pepper

    Prepare the coals. While the fire is getting started prepare the vegetables.
    Cut the onions in half — don't peel them.
    Cut the eggplants in half lengthwise, score the flesh in a crosshatch pattern but do not cut through skin. Salt the eggplant and place cut side down on a double layer of paper towels.
    Cut zucchini in half lengthwise.
    Brush the mushrooms clean.

When coals are hot place onions, cut side down, on grill. Place whole peppers on grill.

Let onions cook until browned on cut side, turn over, drizzle olive oil over, continue to cook until oil bubbles and onions are tender. Large onions will take 45 minutes to 1 hour.

Grill the peppers, turning frequently, until skin is charred all over. Place peppers in a brown paper bag and close. Let peppers cool until they are cool enough to handle.

Remove peppers from bag and peel and seed them. As you peel the peppers, let the juice drain into a bowl. Cut the peppers into 1/2" strips and add to the bowl.

Dress peppers with 1/4 cup olive oil, the sliced garlic, salt and freshly ground black pepper.

Pat the eggplants dry with a paper towel. Place cut side down on grill. When browned, turn flesh side up and drizzle with olive oil. Continue to cook until oil bubbles and flesh is tender.

Place zucchini cut side down on grill, broil until browned, turn and cook the other side. Brush flesh side with olive oil. Eggplant and zucchini will cook quickly, about 10 to 20 minutes, depending on size.

Place mushrooms cap side up on grill. When browned turn stem side up. Drizzle olive oil into cap and continue to cook until oil bubbles. Mushrooms will cook quickly — about 5 to 10 minutes.

Arrange all the vegetables, except the peppers, on a large serving platter and serve. You may serve them hot or at room temperature.

This is a general plan for a mixed grill. The onions and peppers take the longest to cook, so start with them. The onions continue to cook while the peppers steam in the bag. The rest of the vegetables can grill while you peel the peppers. Serves 4 – 6.

A delicious alternative to plain olive oil is a dressing made of:

1/2 to 1/3 cup olive oil
1 - 2 cloves garlic, minced
a handful of basil leaves, chopped
a few sprigs parsley, chopped
salt and freshly ground black pepper

Pour the olive oil into a small bowl. Add the remaining ingredients. Mix well.

After turning the eggplant, drizzle the dressing into the flesh — filling the score marks. Continue cooking until it is bubbly and tender. After turning the zucchini, drizzle or brush on the dressing and continue to cook. After turning the mushrooms, drizzle the mixture into the mushroom caps and continue to cook until they are tender.

You can also cut vegetables in 1/2" slices, brush with olive oil and grill.

Brown one side, turn, and brown the other side. Sliced vegetables will take about 15 minutes to grill.

In the winter I grilled potatoes, turnips, carrots and parsnips on a grill in the fireplace. Delicious!

POTATOES IN FOIL

4-6 medium potatoes
2-3 medium onions
about 1/4 cup butter — more if you wish
salt and freshly ground black pepper
water

Scrub potatoes and slice into 1/4" slices. Slice onions.

Tear off 4 sheets of aluminum foil. Each sheet should be large enough to wrap each individual portion. Divide potatoes and onions equally among the 4 sheets. Dot with butter. Season with salt and pepper.

Wrap foil around potatoes — to make a flat packet. Bring two ends of foil together, crease and fold the edges together 2 or 3 times — so the edges have been enclosed inside the folds. The final fold should be flat and tight against the packet.

Use the same folding method on each of the ends. Before sealing the last end add 1 Tablespoon water. Seal and wrap with a second layer of foil.

Place packets on the grill over hot coals. Cook for about 1 hour — until the packets feel soft and the potatoes are tender. Turn at least once.

Serve individual packets or open and scrape potatoes into a serving bowl.

This is terrific campfire food. You can place packets directly on the coals — keep turning them to prevent scorching.

This is a favorite family recipe.

I've also used this method with small new potatoes. Cut potatoes into quarters or halves. Add 1 or 2 garlic cloves and a few sprigs of rosemary to each packet. Drizzle some olive oil over the potatoes and season with salt and pepper. Cook as above.

GRILLED CORN

6 ears of fresh sweet corn — with husks on but silk removed

Soak corn with husks in a large pan of water for ½ hour.

Prepare the coals.

Place the corn on the hot grill, turning to grill on all sides. It's okay to let the husks brown and blacken a bit.

Cook until heated through — about 10 – 15 minutes, depending on the size of the ears of corn and the heat of the coals. Remove from grill and serve.

Everyone can husk his own ear. This is so tasty you don't need to add butter — but you certainly can if you like.

VEGETABLES

VEGETABLES

I cannot think of a vegetable I don't like. From artichokes to zucchini — they are so varied in taste, shape and texture.

I can make a meal of vegetables and a salad — a baked potato and a salad — or grilled vegetables with a piece of crusty bread to soak up their juices and oil.

Vegetables are so often overcooked that their fresh flavor and color are gone — and they taste watery and bland.

I've included recipes that are not complicated, but are not simply steamed. Try some of the vegetables you've not liked before — you may be surprised!

Broccoli with Oil and Lemon

1 medium bunch of broccoli
juice of one lemon
2-3 Tablespoons good olive oil
1 clove garlic, cut in slices
salt and freshly ground black pepper

Clean the broccoli and cut into medium-sized florets.

Steam until tender.

Transfer to a bowl. Add the lemon and the garlic. Salt and pepper to taste.

This is delicious served warm or at room temperature as a salad.

Serves 3-4.

Artichokes Roman Style

4 large artichokes
juice of 1 lemon
2 Tablespoons mint, chopped
2 Tablespoons parsley, chopped
1-3 cloves garlic, chopped
salt to taste
1/2 cup olive oil

Prepare a large bowl of water and add the lemon juice.

Clean the artichokes by snapping back and pulling down the leaves. The leaves should break off where they become tender. As you get further into the heart, the leaves will break off higher. Eventually a pale cone-shaped yellow heart will be exposed. Cut 1 to 2 inches of the tough tips off the top of the cone. Be ruthless— you want to eliminate all the tough, stringy parts and have a tender, completely edible heart.

Spread the top of the artichoke to find the fuzzy choke. Remove all of this prickly center with a small spoon. The artichoke heart should remain.

Pare away the tough skin from the stem and bottom of the artichoke — do not remove the stem. Drop the prepared artichokes into the lemon water to prevent discoloration.

Mix the mint, parsley, garlic and salt in a small bowl. Mint is traditional, but if I cannot find fresh mint I use a little more parsley.

Drain the artichokes. Pat dry with paper towels.

Spoon some of the herb mixture into the center of each artichoke. Rub some of the mixture on the outside of each one.

Place the artichokes stem side up in a heavy pot that is just large enough to accommodate them and hold them upright. It is okay if a bit of the herb mixture falls into the pan — it will become part of the sauce.

Add the olive oil and enough water to cover the bottom third of the artichokes. Cover and cook over medium low heat until artichokes are tender but firm.

Add water if liquid evaporates too quickly. If sauce is too watery remove cover and continue cooking.

When artichokes are tender transfer to a serving platter.

If the sauce is still watery — cook, uncovered, until it reduces to a syrupy liquid. Cool the artichokes. Pour the juices over them before serving.

Serves 4.

This is a wonderful make-ahead first course. Serve on pretty, small, deep plates and pour the sauce over the artichokes.

It is also a lovely addition to an antipasto platter. Cut the artichokes into quarters and serve with antipasto.

Baked Beets

6 medium beets
3-4 Tablespoons butter or olive oil

Cut the tops off of the beets,
leaving about 1" of stems.
Scrub clean and wrap
in an aluminum
foil packet. Bake
in a 350° oven for
about an hour or until
tender.

Remove from oven, unwrap and cool until cool enough to handle.

Peel skin off and slice.

Sauté in a heavy skillet with butter or oil.

Serve at once.

Serves 4.

Or slice and cool. Pour vinaigrette dressing, on page 164, over and gently toss. These beets are a great addition to a platter of vegetables — celeriac remoulade, shredded carrots, cucumbers and dill.

Baking beets is easy and gives the beets a richer flavor than boiling. I use this method to prepare beets for any recipe that calls for cooked beets.

Mushrooms with Garlic, Basil and Parsley

1– 1½ pounds mushrooms
⅓ cup olive oil
1– 2 cloves garlic, cut in half
1– 2 Tablespoons parsley, chopped
1– 2 Tablespoons basil, chopped
salt and freshly ground black pepper

Clean the mushrooms. Do not clean in water. Use a mushroom brush or a damp paper towel.

Slice the mushroom ¼" thick.

Pour the oil into a large, heavy skillet. Add the garlic and sauté until it becomes

126

golden. Do not burn the garlic.

Add the mushrooms and cook over medium high heat. Toss and stir until the mushrooms begin to absorb the oil. Turn the heat down a bit and continue to cook — stirring and tossing — until the mushrooms release their juices. Turn the heat back to medium high and sauté until the mushrooms are cooked and the juices have almost cooked away.

Add the chopped herbs. Season with salt and freshly ground black pepper.

Serve immediately.

Serves 4.

Mushrooms prepared this way are very good in frittata, page 246.

Eggplant with Onions

2-3 small eggplants
1/3 cup olive oil
2 cloves garlic, cut in half
2 medium onions, sliced
salt and freshly ground black pepper
basil and parsley, chopped

Wash eggplants and slice 1/4" thick. Place in a colander and sprinkle with salt. Toss with your hands to distribute the salt. Place colander in the sink or in a large bowl. Let eggplant drain for 20 minutes. Pat the eggplant dry with paper towels.

In a heavy iron skillet heat the oil over medium high heat. Add garlic and onions and cook until golden.

Add the eggplant. Toss to coat the eggplant with the oil and onion mixture. The eggplant will quickly absorb the oil.

If the eggplant seems to be browning too quickly, turn heat down. Continue to cook. The eggplant will release some juices and oil as it cooks. Continue to cook until the eggplant is tender— about 15 – 20 minutes — less if the eggplants are young and tender.

Season with salt and pepper. Add the chopped basil and parsley to taste. Toss a minute or two and serve.

Serves 4.

I like to use small, slender eggplants for this dish. I don't peel the skins because they are usually quite tender.

It is possible to use large eggplants. Peel, then dice and place in the colander.

Sometimes I add sliced zucchini to the eggplants and onions. You can also add chopped tomatoes and sliced sweet peppers. Or combine them all for a summer medley. I use whatever vegetables

I find in the garden. Be sure to use generous amounts of basil.

Whatever combination you use will make a lovely side dish. The vegetables can also be used as a base for frittata.

Vegetables prepared this way will freeze well. When the garden is overflowing I cook up a large batch and spoon it into plastic freezer bags.

On a cold winter day I slip the vegetables out of the bag and into a shallow baking dish. Place in a 350° oven and bake for about 30 minutes. The vegetables should begin to cook and soften. Spread them evenly in the dish and bake for another 15 to 20 minutes —until they are warmed through and the moisture has evaporated.

I sometimes make a quick meal of this by adding a few slices of mozzarella and some freshly grated Parmesan cheese after I've spread the vegetables in the dish. Bake until the cheese is browned and crusty— about 15 to 20 minutes.

Zucchini with Garlic

3-4 small zucchini
1/3 cup olive oil
2 cloves garlic, cut in half
Salt and freshly ground black pepper
1 Tablespoon chopped parsley
1 Tablespoon chopped basil

Scrub the zucchini and slice 1/8" thick or less. The best zucchini are the very small ones.

In a heavy skillet heat the olive oil over medium high heat. Add the garlic and cook until garlic becomes golden. Do not burn garlic.

Add the sliced zucchini. Toss to coat zucchini with oil. Toss and stir until zucchini is tender but not soft. If the zucchini are small and fresh they will cook in a few minutes. Salt and pepper to taste. Add the chopped parsley and basil and cook for a minute or so. Serve immediately. Serves 4.

Stuffed Eggplant

2 - 3 medium eggplants
3 - 4 Tablespoons olive oil
1 - 2 medium onions, chopped
1 clove garlic, finely chopped
3/4 pound mushrooms, chopped
1 - 2 medium tomatoes, peeled, seeded and
                              chopped
salt and freshly ground black pepper
Parmesan cheese, grated

Cut eggplants in half lengthwise. Sprinkle with salt and place cut side down on a double layer of paper towels. Drain for 20 minutes. Pat dry. Carefully scoop out the pulp — do not puncture the skin.

Coarsely chop the eggplant.

Pour oil into a large, heavy skillet. Add the onions and the garlic. Sauté for a few minutes, until onions become golden. Add the chopped eggplant and mushrooms. Sauté a few more minutes.

Add tomatoes and cook until mixture is soft — about 10 minutes.

Salt and pepper to taste.

Fill the eggplant shells with the eggplant mixture. Sprinkle with the Parmesan cheese.

Bake at 350° for 30 to 40 minutes. The eggplants should be heated through and the cheese browned and bubbly.

Serve hot or at room temperature.

Serves 4 – 6.

BAKED SQUASH

Acorn and small butternut or buttercup squash work well in this recipe.

1 – 2 squash — allow 1 squash for 2 servings
2 – 4 Tablespoons butter
nutmeg, optional
salt and freshly ground black pepper

Cut squash in half lengthwise and scoop out the seeds.

Select a baking pan that will hold the squash halves face down and flat. Pour 1/4" water in the pan.

Bake at 350° until squash begins to get tender. Turn cut side up and add a chunk of butter to each squash cavity.

Grate a little nutmeg, if desired. Season with salt and pepper. Continue to bake until the squash is tender and browned.

Serves 2 – 4.

PURÉED BUTTERNUT SQUASH

1 large butternut squash
salt to taste
2-3 Tablespoons butter
freshly ground black pepper, optional
freshly grated nutmeg, optional

Peel and cut squash into 1" cubes. Place in a heavy pot and add 1/4" water. Add salt. Cover and bring to a boil. Turn heat down and simmer until squash is tender — about 20-25 minutes. Make sure the squash does not dry out while cooking — but do not add water unless it is necessary. When squash is tender, drain and put pot back on the heat for a few minutes to dry excess moisture.

Mash squash or purée in a food processor. Add the butter. Taste for salt. Add the pepper and nutmeg if desired. Pour into a serving bowl; top with an additional pat of butter. Serve hot. Serves 4—6.

Roasted Vegetables

Almost any vegetable can be roasted. Normally we think of potatoes, but all root vegetables are delicious — parsnips, carrots, beets, turnips — as well as potatoes. Onions, leeks and spring onions are also tasty. Fennel has an entirely different taste when roasted. Tomatoes are wonderful when slowly roasted.

You can roast vegetables singly or in combination. Potatoes and onions are a classic combination. I love this with a bit of rosemary or sage.

Parsnips and carrots roasted together are a sweet combination. A medley of root vegetables in all their subdued colors is wonderful.

I use olive oil for brushing the vegetables. I also use herb flavored oils to add an herbal flavor — or add a few sprigs of rosemary, sage or thyme to vegetables along with the salt and pepper.

To roast root vegetables:

Select 2 or 3 vegetables per serving of the following:

potatoes
carrots
parsnips
turnips
beets
onions
1 - 2 Tablespoons olive oil
salt and freshly ground black pepper

Peel and cut the vegetables into 2" to 3" pieces. Brush with oil or put them in a bowl and toss with oil until all the pieces are coated. Season with salt and pepper.

Put the vegetables in a heavy roasting pan that can accommodate them without crowding, so they will roast and not steam.

Roast at 350° until the vegetables are crusty and golden on the outside and tender on the inside — about 45 minutes to 1 hour.

To roast small whole onions:

8–12 small white onions
2–3 Tablespoons olive oil
Salt and freshly ground black pepper
½ cup balsamic vinegar

Toss the onions in the oil and roast as above. When they are browned and tender — about 25–35 minutes — remove them from the roasting pan. Add the balsamic vinegar to the pan and cook over medium heat. Scrape any loose residue in the bottom of the pan and mix into the vinegar. Reduce the vinegar; when it has thickened, pour it over the onions. Toss the onions in the sauce and serve. Serves 4.

To roast fennel:

2 large fennel bulbs
2–3 Tablespoons olive oil
salt and freshly ground black pepper

Peel away any brown spots or tough parts of the fennel. Trim off the stems. Cut each bulb into wedges. Toss in the olive oil and season with salt and pepper.

Roast as above. Cook until the fennel is tender — about 15 to 20 minutes.

Serves 4.

You can top the fennel with some freshly grated Parmesan cheese — after it is tender. Put under the broiler for a few minutes to brown the cheese.

To roast tomatoes:

2 – 4 large, ripe tomatoes
1 clove garlic, minced
1 Tablespoon basil, chopped
1 teaspoon parsley, chopped
salt and freshly ground black pepper
2 – 3 Tablespoons olive oil

Cut tomatoes in half. Place in a heavy roasting pan with cut side up. Sprinkle tomatoes with garlic, basil, parsley, salt and pepper. Drizzle the olive oil on top.

Roast at low heat — 300° for 1½ to 2 hours. The tomatoes should cook slowly until some of the juices have cooked away and the tomato is browned. Serve hot or at room temperature.

Serves 4 – 6.

GLAZED PARSNIPS

6-8 medium parsnips
1/4 cup butter
1-2 teaspoons brown sugar or maple syrup
2 Tablespoons Dijon mustard
2-3 Tablespoons Bourbon
salt and freshly ground black pepper

Clean and peel the parsnips. Cut in half or quarters lengthwise. Steam until almost tender — about 10 minutes. Do not overcook. Drain the parsnips.

Combine the butter, brown sugar or maple syrup, mustard and Bourbon in a small sauce pan. Cook over low heat until slightly thickened.

Place parsnips in a shallow, buttered baking dish. Pour the sauce over. Salt and pepper to taste.

Bake at 350° for 15 to 20 minutes until the parsnips are browned and bubbly. Serve at once.

Serves 4-6.

SAUTÉED SPINACH

2-3 large bunches spinach
1 clove garlic, cut in half
2-3 Tablespoons olive oil
1-2 rosemary sprigs

Wash the spinach in lots of water. If the leaves are crinkly, you may want to wash the spinach twice to get rid of any sand that might be lurking in those deep folds. Remove any tough stems.

In a large, heavy skillet sauté the garlic in the oil. Do not let the garlic burn. When garlic begins to color add the rosemary and the spinach.

Toss until spinach is coated with oil. Continue to toss and cook until spinach is wilted and turns bright green.

Remove garlic and rosemary and serve at once.

Serves 4.

Potatoes

MASHED POTATOES

6-8 medium potatoes
1/2 to 1 cup hot milk
6 Tablespoons butter
salt to taste

    Peel and cut potatoes into 2" pieces. Place in a pot and add water and salt. Bring to a boil, turn down and cook until potatoes are tender — about 20 minutes.
    Drain — reserve the water, if you like, for soups — and put pot back on heat to dry up the last bit of water.
    I like to pass the potatoes through a food mill and then transfer them to a large mixing bowl.
    Heat milk and add slowly to the potatoes, whipping with a fork or a whisk. Continue to add milk and whip until potatoes are soft, fluffy and moist. Potatoes tend to dry out a bit before they are served — so be sure they are moist enough. Add

the butter and taste for salt. Transfer to a pan to keep warm over very low heat.

Pour into a warm serving bowl and top with a large pat of butter. Serve at once.

Serves 4 - 6.

Sometimes instead of milk I use the potato water for liquid and olive oil instead of butter. Follow the method above. Reserve the potato water and add it gradually as you whip the potatoes. Try cooking a clove or two of garlic along with the potatoes. Top with olive oil that has chopped basil added to it.

BAKED POTATOES

1 large baking potato for each serving
optional:
> butter or
> sour cream or
> yogurt
> chopped chives

Scrub potatoes and pierce a few times with a fork. Bake at 425° for about 1 hour.

I like the skins to get really crisp and crunchy and the potatoes soft. If you prefer them less crispy bake at 375° - 400°.

I often speed up the process by putting potatoes in the microwave for 6 to 8 minutes or until they begin to soften. Then transfer potatoes to a hot oven for 10 to 15 minutes to continue the baking and to crisp up the skins.

Serve with butter, sour cream or yogurt and chopped chives, if desired. I find a bit of freshly ground black pepper is tasty and far less fattening.

New Potatoes with Parsley and Butter

12 – 16 new small potatoes
1/4 cup butter
2 – 3 Tablespoons chopped parsley
salt and freshly ground black pepper

Scrub the potatoes. If they are large cut them in half. Place the potatoes in a heavy saucepan and add about 1/2" water. Add salt. Bring to a boil, then turn down heat and cook, covered, until potatoes are tender — about 15 – 20 minutes.

If there is water in the pan, remove the cover and cook until water evaporates. Taste for salt.

Add the butter and let it melt over the potatoes. Add the chopped parsley and a few grindings of black pepper.

Gently toss the potatoes to cover with butter and parsley. Pour into a warm bowl and serve at once. Serves 4.

Roasted Potatoes with Rosemary and Garlic

12 - 16 small new potatoes
garlic cloves — a few for flavor or a dozen
or more if you plan to serve roasted
garlic
1/4 cup olive oil
a few sprigs of rosemary
salt and freshly ground black pepper

Scrub the potatoes — do not peel. Put potatoes in a heavy ovenproof casserole with a lid. Add garlic, oil and rosemary. Add salt and pepper to taste.

Cover and bake at 450° for about 1 hour. The potatoes should be crispy and tender on the inside.

You may want to toss the potatoes a few times while they are cooking.

This is a terrific potato dish — and it's easy! It is especially good with roast chicken or lamb.

Serve the garlic cloves with the potatoes. The long baking sweetens them. Put the cloves between your teeth and squeeze the garlic out of their skins.

You may replace the rosemary with a few sage leaves for a different herbal flavor.

Serves 4-6.

Crispy Fried Potatoes

6 to 8 medium potatoes
1/2 cup olive oil
salt

Scrub potatoes and cut into 3/4" cubes.
In a large, heavy iron skillet, heat the oil. There should be enough oil to generously fill the bottom of the skillet. When oil is hot, pat potatoes dry and add them to the oil. Toss until the potatoes are covered with oil.

Turn heat to medium and cook, uncovered, until potatoes are golden brown and crusty on the outside and tender on the inside. This should take 20-30 minutes. If the potatoes are browning before they are tender, turn the heat down and continue to cook.

Salt to taste. Toss. Serve immediately. Serves 6.

You may add a garlic clove or a sprig of rosemary to the potatoes.

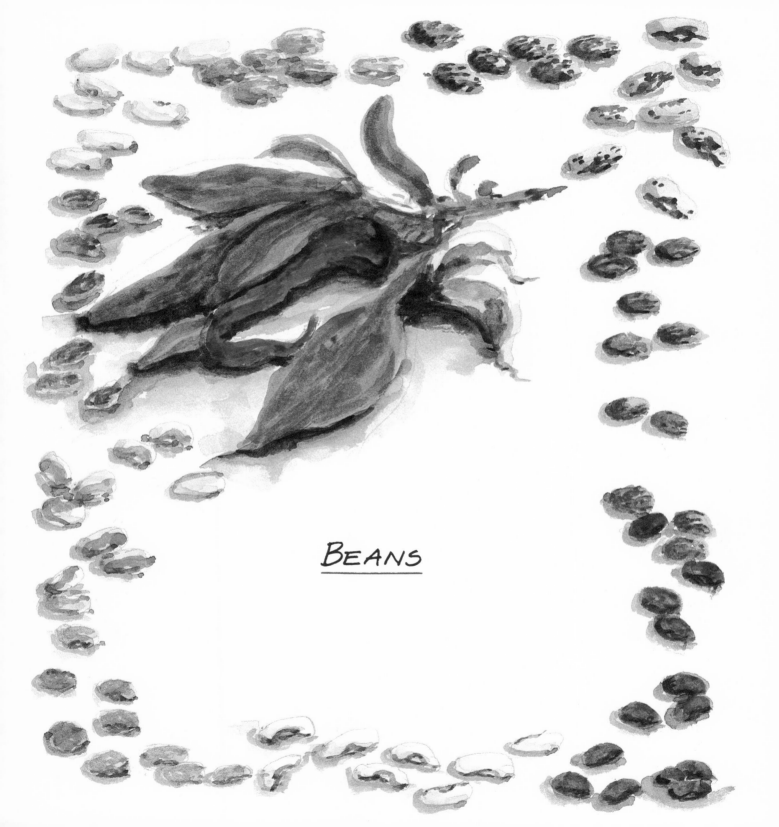

Beans

COOKING DRIED BEANS

Place the beans in a bowl and cover with water—about 2" to 3" above the beans. Soak overnight.

Rinse and drain the beans. Remove any that have not expanded and any stones or other foreign matter.

Place the beans in a heavy pot and cover with water — about 2" above the beans.

Bring the beans to a boil. Turn down heat, cover and cook at a very low simmer. Do not allow beans to boil hard. The beans should retain their shape. Cook until beans are tender. Cooking time will vary depending on the type of beans and how fresh they are. Plan on 2 to 3 hours.

The beans are now ready to be used for any recipe calling for cooked beans.

If you don't have time to soak the beans you can place beans in the pot, cover with water and bring to a boil. Boil for 2 minutes, cover and let stand for 1 hour, and proceed.

Tuscan Beans

1 pound cannellini beans
   or other white dried
   beans
4-5 sage leaves
2 garlic cloves, peeled
   and left whole
2-3 Tablespoons olive
         oil
additional olive oil for
    serving

   Soak beans
overnight in lots
of water. Rinse
and eliminate
any beans
that have not
expanded.
   Place the
beans in a

153

heavy pot and cover with water — by about 2".

Add sage leaves, garlic and olive oil.

Place over very low heat and simmer very slowly for about 3 hours. The beans should be tender but firm. Add salt to taste.

Serve the beans as a side dish. In Florence they are served with grilled steak or grilled chicken.

Pass the olive oil and drizzle on top. Be generous with the oil — and be sure to use a good fruity virgin olive oil!

Serves 8—10.

Lima beans are delicious cooked this way. Cook only until tender, 20 to 30 minutes. Pass the olive oil.

Any dried bean can be cooked this way, but the cannellini are the classic Italian beans.

Tuscan Beans with Tomatoes

½ cup olive oil
6-7 sage leaves
4 cloves garlic, cut in half
6 medium tomatoes, peeled, seeded and chopped
      or one 16 ounce can peeled Italian
      tomatoes
salt and freshly ground black pepper
4 cups cooked cannellini beans, page 153

Heat olive oil in a heavy pan. Add sage and garlic. Sauté on medium heat 4 to 5 minutes. Add tomatoes. If using canned tomatoes pass through a food mill to remove the seeds.

Season with salt and pepper. Simmer, uncovered, for 10-15 minutes.

Add the beans. Stir well and cook 15 to 20 minutes more.

Serve hot. Serves 4-6.

Baked Beans

2 cups dried beans — navy, pinto, cranberry
even lima beans are good

salt to taste
1/2 — 1 teaspoon dry mustard
1/2 cup maple syrup
1/2 pound salt pork
1—2 medium onions

Soak beans overnight. Drain and rinse. Put in a heavy pot and cover with water. Simmer over low heat until beans become tender, and the skin puckers and bursts when you blow on it. Salt to taste.

Scoop beans into bean pot. Reserve any remaining cooking water. Add the remaining ingredients. The salt pork can be left whole or cut into pieces. The onions may be left whole or cut into wedges.

Mix until seasonings are blended. Add enough cooking liquid to cover beans.

Cover and cook in a slow oven at 300° until beans are tender and browned. It should take about 4 hours. Add reserved liquid if beans begin to dry out.

All the seasonings can be adjusted to taste — use more or less maple syrup, etc. Also, if you like you may add ketchup — about 1/2 cup — with the rest of the seasonings.

Serves 6-8.

White Bean Salad

3 cups cooked cannellini beans or other
              white beans, see recipe on page 152
1 large sweet onion, thinly sliced
1/2 cup good olive oil
1 Tablespoon red wine vinegar
salt and freshly ground black pepper
1-2 Tablespoons chopped parsley
1 Tablespoon chopped basil

    Put the beans in a serving bowl. Add onion, oil and vinegar and toss gently. Season with salt and pepper. Sprinkle chopped parsley and basil on top. Toss again, gently.
    Serve — or let marinate for a few hours and then serve at room temperature.
    You may substitute canned cannellini beans — rinse and drain first.
    You may add one 7 ounce can of Italian tuna packed in oil with the rest of the ingredients for a more substantial salad.

158

Lentil Salad

1 pound lentils
5 cups water
2 teaspoons salt
1/2 cup olive oil
1 large onion, chopped

for the dressing, mix together:
1/2 cup olive oil
2 Tablespoons wine vinegar
salt and freshly ground black pepper
2 Tablespoons chopped parsley for garnish

Place lentils and water in a heavy covered saucepan. Add salt. Bring to a boil and cook, covered, over medium heat for 20 to 25 minutes. The lentils should be tender but not mushy. Drain well.

Put lentils in a large bowl. Add olive oil and toss gently. Cool.

When cool add the onion and the dressing. Toss gently. Let mellow in the refrigerator. Garnish with chopped parsley.

SALADS

SALADS

I love bitter greens — arugula, chicory, escarole and frisée — and often serve one of them alone or mixed with other greens.

The Italian "tricolore" salad — arugula, radicchio and endive — is another favorite.

The French salad — mild butterhead lettuce with a mustardy vinaigrette — is also delicious.

Another choice is mesclun (French) or misticanza (Italian). This is a mix of baby greens. These are easy to grow — even in a few pots on a terrace. Mix seeds of arugula, rachicchio, frisée and cress along with seeds of some mild lettuces — romaine, red leaf, butterhead, cutting lettuces and perhaps some chervil. Scatter seeds over soil and cover lightly with soil. Water lightly.

When greens are 3" to 4" tall cut them, leaving 1" on the plants. Water with a bit of fertilizer added, and the greens will grow back again.

The basic rules for a good salad:

1. The greens should be fresh, washed and spun dry — or dried in clean tea towels.
2. Toss the salad just before serving.
3. Use a high quality oil — virgin olive oil is best.
4. Use a good wine vinegar —red or white.
5. Toss salad gently until all the leaves are covered with oil.

   The proportion of oil to vinegar will depend on the strength of the vinegar. Use enough to add tartness — but not so much as to give a strong vinegar flavor.
   An old Italian proverb calls for four people to make a good salad:
   a just person to add the salt
   a generous person to add the oil
   a stingy person to add the vinegar
   a patient person to toss it all

163

I make the dressing while I'm preparing the meal, then add the greens
just before serving — usually after the
main course.

VINAIGRETTE

½ teaspoon salt — or to taste
½ teaspoon dry mustard
1 clove garlic, peeled and cut in half
¼ cup olive oil
1 – 1½ teaspoon vinegar
freshly ground black pepper

In a large salad bowl, sprinkle the
salt — coarse kosher salt is best. Add the
mustard. Add the garlic halves. Use a
fork to slightly crush the garlic and rub
it into the mustard and salt. If you like
a mild garlic flavor, only slightly crush
the garlic — if you want a strong garlic
taste, crush and mash it into the salt
and mustard.

Add the oil and mix. Add the vinegar and beat with a fork until well blended.

The dressing is now ready. If it sits for a while — it will need to be mixed again before adding the greens. Discard any pieces of garlic before adding the greens. Add freshly ground pepper before tossing.

This is a simple dressing with a touch of garlic. The amounts are approximate — taste the dressing until you have the correct proportions.

If you want a more mustardy vinaigrette add a teaspoon or more — to taste — of a good Dijon mustard. This is especially good on frisée or butterhead lettuce.

If you add balsamic vinegar instead of wine vinegar, you will have a slightly sweeter, less acidic dressing.

You may use the juice of 1/2 lemon instead of the vinegar for a very fresh and slightly tart dressing.

This will make enough dressing for a large bowl of salad greens — enough for 4 to 6.

CELERIAC REMOULADE

1 large knob celeriac —
    1 to 1¼ pounds
1 recipe for mustardy
    vinaigrette, page 165

    Put celeriac through
the medium shredding
disc of the food processor.
Or grate on a medium-
sized grater. Place in
a bowl. Pour boiling water
over it. Let stand for
1 minute. Pour off hot
water. Pour cold
water over it,
drain and cool.
    When cool — pour on
mustardy vinaigrette made
with lemon and Dijon mustard.
    Chill. Let stand in the refrigerator
for at least a few hours before serving.

This can also be served with a mustardy mayonnaise:

Add 2-3 teaspoons Dijon mustard to 1/3 to 1/2 cup good mayonnaise and mix with prepared celeriac.

I prefer the lighter taste of the vinaigrette — but both dressings are delicious.

FENNEL SALAD

1 or 2 large fennel
1 recipe basic vinaigrette, page 164

Wash the fennel, cut off the top leaves. You may reserve a few of the feathery leaves for garnish. Cut away any brownish spots or any tough parts.

Cut fennel in quarters — stem to root. Remove the tough core. Then beginning at the root end, cut into thin slices.

Toss in a bowl with vinaigrette dressing. Serves 3 — 4.

Fennel is delicious on its own as a winter salad. It is also tasty mixed with julienned bright red peppers — a beautiful color combination.

It is also wonderful in a mixed green salad, especially with arugula — the tangy arugula and the slightly sweet aniselike fennel complement each other.

SHREDDED CARROT SALAD

3–4 large carrots, about 1 to 1¼ pounds
1 recipe lemon vinaigrette dressing, page 164

Shred the carrots in the food processor or on a medium-sized grater.
Add the lemon vinaigrette and toss.
Serves 4.

This is a refreshing salad – especially good for lunch on a combination salad plate of shredded carrots, sliced cucumbers with dill, celeriac remoulade, sliced beets and a radish or two.
In French bistros this is called "assiette des crudités" or plate of raw vegetables.

Green Bean Salad

1 pound fresh green beans
1 medium onion, sliced
1 recipe vinaigrette dressing, page 164

Trim, wash and stem the beans. Cook until bright green and tender. Refresh the beans by pouring cold water over them
Drain and place in a serving bowl. Add the vinaigrette and toss.
Top with sliced onions and serve.
Serves 4.

The lemony vinaigrette, page 165, is also delicious with beans. You can eliminate the onions if you like. Fresh herbs chopped and added with the dressing add a good flavor. I especially like chopped dill.

Cucumbers with Dill

2 cucumbers
salt
1 recipe for vinaigrette dressing, page 164
   or ¼–½ cup mayonnaise, sour cream or yogurt
4–6 dill sprigs, chopped
     and a few sprigs for garnish
salt and freshly ground black pepper

Peel and halve the cucumbers lengthwise. Scoop out the seeds, and discard.

Thinly slice by hand or on thin slicer of a food processor.

Put cucumbers into a colander and sprinkle with salt. Toss with your hands to mix salt and cucumbers. Place colander in the sink or large bowl to drain for 20 to 25 minutes.

Squeeze the liquid from the cucumbers and put them in a bowl.

Add the vinaigrette and chopped dill. Toss well. Salt and pepper to taste.

Instead of vinaigrette you may use a good mayonnaise or sour cream or a mixture of both. Yogurt is also good — and less fattening.

Chill until ready to serve. Sprinkle with chopped dill or a few dill sprigs.

This is a terrific summer salad — great for picnics. Delicious with poached salmon.

TOMATOES AND BASIL

2 – 3 large, fresh, ripe tomatoes
12 – 15 basil leaves
2 – 3 Tablespoons olive oil
salt and freshly ground black pepper

Slice the tomatoes 1/2" thick. Arrange on a serving platter.

Chop, shred or tear basil leaves and sprinkle on top. To shred basil, stack 10 – 12 leaves and thinly slice with a very sharp knife.

Pour olive oil on top. You may add a touch of vinegar — red wine or balsamic.

Season with salt and pepper.

Serves 3 – 4.

In the summer, when the tomatoes are ripe, this can be lunch or supper for me. Add some freshly baked bread and a glass of wine.

174

TOMATO, CUCUMBER, ONION AND BASIL SALAD

2-3 medium, ripe, firm tomatoes
1 cucumber
1 large sweet onion
2-3 Tablespoons olive oil
2-3 teaspoons vinegar
6-8 basil leaves, shredded or chopped
salt and freshly ground black pepper

Cut the tomatoes into wedges. Peel the cucumber, cut in half lengthwise, scoop out the seeds and discard them. Cut the cucumbers into chunks. Cut the onion into wedges.

Put all the vegetables into a bowl. Add oil and vinegar. Toss to mix. Season with shredded basil, salt and pepper.

Serve at once.

Serves 4.

You may also add an avocado — cut into chunks — to this salad.

Salad Caprese
Mozzarella, Tomato and Basil

3-4 large, ripe, firm tomatoes
1 pound fresh mozzarella
20-25 basil leaves
1/4 - 1/3 cup fruity olive oil
salt and freshly ground black
    pepper

Slice the tomatoes fairly thick—about 1/2". Slice the mozzarella into 1/4" slices.

Arrange the tomatoes and mozzarella on a platter, alternating slices.

Place basil leaves between tomato and mozzarella slices. Or shred basil leaves by stacking them on top of each other and slicing into thin slices with a very sharp knife. Sprinkle shredded basil over tomatoes and cheese.

Drizzle olive oil over top. Don't skimp on the oil.

Serve with a good, crusty fresh bread to soak up the olive oil and tomato juices.

Serve immediately.

Serves 4-6.

Salad Frisée

2 small heads frisée
4-6 slices thick bacon
crostini, see page 9
1 small goat cheese
1 recipe mustardy vinaigrette, page 165

Wash and spin dry frisée — a small curly endive — or you may use the inner pale hearts of large heads of endive.

Cut the bacon crosswise into 1/2" strips. Cook over medium heat until bacon is done and is just beginning to crisp. Drain on paper towels.

Cut bread for crostini. Oil the bread and place on cookie sheet. Broil one side — turn crostini over and place a 1/4" slice of goat cheese on each crostini. Broil until the cheese bubbles and is golden brown — about 2 to 3 minutes.

Toss the greens with the vinaigrette. Sprinkle bacon pieces on top. Place crostini on top of salad. Serve immediately.

Serves 3-4.

As an alternative to the crostini boil new potatoes — cut in half and top with goat cheese slices. Broil until cheese bubbles and browns.

Any way you serve this, it is a wonderful salad meal.

179

Cole Slaw

1 large head cabbage, shredded
2-3 carrots, shredded
1/2 cup white wine vinegar
3 Tablespoons sugar
1 teaspoon salt
1 Tablespoon Dijon mustard
2/3 cup olive oil

   Combine cabbage and carrots in a large earthenware or glass bowl. Toss.
   In a small bowl, mix the remaining ingredients. Whisk together. Pour dressing over the vegetables and toss to mix. Cover with plastic wrap and chill for 2-3 hours before serving. I like the cabbage to be slightly wilted.
   My mother made her cole slaw with a cream dressing. Use the same amounts of vinegar, sugar and salt. Substitute cream for the oil. Eliminate the mustard.

BREADS

BREADS

My mother taught my sisters and me how to bake bread along with all the other baking projects we had each summer for our 4-H projects. We learned how to bake cookies, cakes, pies, bread and countless other things.

Bread is so satisfying to make. There is nothing like kneading bread dough into a smooth and elastic mass. It can be very therapeutic — a lot of tension seems to be kneaded out along with the bread. And there is truly nothing like the smell of fresh bread baking!

Bread freezes well. Wrap loaves in airtight aluminum foil or put in plastic freezer bags. To thaw, remove bread from wrappings and thaw on a rack. For a freshly baked taste warm the bread through in a 350° oven. Plan on 5 to 10 minutes for small loaves and 15 to 20 minutes for large ones.

Gloria's White Bread

4 cups lukewarm water
1 package or 2 teaspoons dry yeast
1 Tablespoon salt
6-8 cups unbleached flour

Pour water into a large mixing bowl. Add the yeast and stir until dissolved.

Add half of the flour and the salt. Beat well. Add the remaining flour and mix with a wooden spoon until dough forms.

If you have trouble incorporating all the flour, turn dough out on to a bread board or clean counter that has been lightly floured.

Mix and knead until the flour is incorporated. The amount of flour is approximate — you may not need all 8 cups.

Continue to knead until dough is smooth and elastic — about 10 minutes.

Place dough in an oiled bowl and cover with a damp tea towel. Let rise for about 2 hours or until it has doubled in bulk.

Punch down and shape into loaves.

Gloria, my sister-in-law, makes beautiful braided loaves and brushes them with a beaten egg before baking. They are wonderful golden brown braids.

You may form this dough into any shape you like. Use a bread pan, or shape dough into long, thin baguettes or into a round peasant loaf.

This recipe will make 3-4 loaves in 9" x 5" pans. It will make 6-8 baguettes.

If using bread pans, let rise 30 to 40 minutes or until it has doubled and bake.

If shaping into free-form loaves — let rise 30 to 40 minutes, slash the loaves on top and bake. A round loaf is generally slashed in a cross, and the long loaves are slashed diagonally across the top.

Bake at 375° for 30 to 40 minutes for large loaves and 20 to 25 minutes for small, thin ones. Cool loaves on a cooling rack.

The bread is done if it sounds hollow when thumped.

I like to use a baking stone — it gives the bread a crusty bottom.

If you decide to use a baking stone — form the loaves and let them rise. There should be plenty of flour underneath them so they can easily be picked up or slid onto a bread paddle.

Sprinkle ample cornmeal on a wooden bread paddle and gently lift a loaf onto the paddle. The cornmeal will act as mini ball bearings as you slide the loaves from the paddle onto the baking stone.

I often substitute whole wheat flour for part of the flour. Experiment using different flours — but always keep half white flour, as it has more gluten and will rise better. I always use unbleached flour.

OLD-FASHIONED WHITE BREAD

3 Tablespoons butter or 2 Tablespoons
       butter and 1 Tablespoon lard
3 Tablespoons sugar
1 teaspoon salt
1 cup boiling water
1 cup milk, scalded
1 package yeast
1/4 cup lukewarm water
5 cups flour

Put butter, lard, sugar and salt in a large bowl. Add water and milk and cool to lukewarm. Dissolve yeast in 1/4 cup lukewarm water. Stir into cooled milk mixture. Add 3 cups flour and beat well. Add enough flour to make a soft dough. Knead until smooth. Place in an oiled bowl and cover with a damp tea towel. Let rise until doubled in bulk.

Punch down. Divide in half and shape into 2 loaves. Place in 5"x 9" loaf pans. Bake at 375° until golden brown and bread sounds hollow when tapped — about 1 hour. Makes 2 loaves.

Aunt Esther's Oatmeal Bread

1 cup quick cooking oatmeal
1 Tablespoon salt
2 Tablespoons vegetable oil
2 cups boiling water
1 package dry yeast
1/2 cup sugar
1/2 cup lukewarm water
6 cups unbleached flour

Put oatmeal, salt and oil in a large mixing bowl. Pour boiling water over and mix. Let stand until lukewarm.

187

Dissolve yeast and sugar in lukewarm water. Add it to lukewarm oatmeal mixture. Add 3 cups flour and beat in. Add the remaining flour and mix.

Knead on a floured board or counter-top until dough is smooth and elastic. Place in an oiled bowl and cover with a damp tea towel. Let rise until doubled in bulk — about 2 hours. Shape into loaves. Let rise until doubled.

Bake at 375° for about 45 minutes, until golden brown and when loaf is thumped, it sounds hollow.

This soft bread is best baked in 9"x5" bread pans. It will make 2 loaves.

It makes marvelous toast — especially when it is thick and spread with plenty of butter and jam!

This bread also makes wonderful tea sandwiches. Thinly slice the bread and coat slices with butter or mayonnaise. Top with thinly sliced cucumbers or tomato and cover with another slice of bread. Cut into 3 finger sandwiches.

Zella's Bran Rolls

1 cup vegetable oil
1/2 cup brown sugar
1 1/2 teaspoon salt
1 cup shredded bran cereal
1 cup boiling water
2 packages dry yeast
1 cup lukewarm water
2 eggs, beaten
6-7 cups unbleached flour

Pour oil, sugar, salt and bran into a large mixing bowl. Pour in the boiling water. Mix and let cool.

Dissolve the yeast in the lukewarm water. Stir.

189

When the bran mixture is lukewarm, add the yeast and the eggs.

Add 3 cups of flour and beat. Add the remaining flour and mix in. If dough is too soft add a little more flour. This should be a soft dough.

Knead on a floured board or counter-top until smooth. Put in an oiled bowl and cover with a damp tea towel. Refrigerate overnight or until ready to use. This is a light dough and it rises rapidly. It should double in bulk in less than 2 hours. It can be shaped anytime after that. It will keep in the refrigerator for a week.

My mother used to divide the dough into 4 sections and roll each into a 15" to 18" round about 1/2" thick. She cut each round into 16 pie-shaped wedges and rolled them from the widest to the pointed end to make a crescent or butterhorn shape.

You may make round buns or shape dough into loaves.

Let rolls rise until doubled in bulk.

Bake at 400° – 425° for about 15 minutes or until golden brown.

These rolls are best reheated before serving. Makes 64 rolls.

This is my mother's recipe and these rolls are famous! She was given this recipe when she attended cooking classes when I was a baby. These rolls have been so well liked that the recipe has passed from aunts to cousins to friends. They have traveled all over the country! They were even part of a fund-raising project that my sister, Marianne, started with her youth group, who baked dozens and dozens of these rolls along with other breads to sell.

Sweet Rolls

3/4 cup milk
1/2 cup butter
2 packages dry yeast
1 cup lukewarm water
1/2 cup sugar
1 teaspoon salt
2 eggs, beaten
4-5 cups unbleached flour

Scald the milk and add the butter. Cool to lukewarm. Dissolve the yeast in the luke-warm water. In a large bowl combine the liquid ingredients. Add the sugar, salt, eggs and half of the flour. Beat well. Add the remaining flour. Mix until all the flour is absorbed. The dough should be soft— but you may need to add more flour to it if it is sticky.

Turn onto a floured board or countertop and knead until smooth and elastic.

192

Cover with a damp tea towel and let rise until doubled in bulk.

Punch down and let rise again until almost doubled.

Shape into rolls and let rise until almost doubled.

Bake at 375° – 400° for 12 – 15 minutes or until golden brown.

Makes 30 to 36 rolls.

These are sweet rolls. I use them to make the Christmas rolls — the pecan butterscotch rolls and the orange wreath rolls. See recipes on pages 286, 288.

FOCACCIA

Focaccia is a thin, flat crusty bread—usually baked on a hearth. You can bake it on a baking stone or in a baking pan.

It is best served warm from the oven—terrific for an appetizer while the rest of the meal is being prepared. It is also great for picnics, snacks or as table bread.

I use Gloria's basic bread recipe for focaccia, see page 183. Sometimes I add 1/2 cup of olive oil if I want a richer bread. Add the oil before you add the last half of the flour.

Let rise until doubled.

When dough is ready to shape divide into 8 pieces. Shape each one into a flat round disc. It can be as thick or thin as you like. I like it fairly thick — between 1/2" to 3/4." Place on baking sheets.

Let the focaccia rise for 30 minutes.

If you are using a baking stone gently transfer a focaccia to a bread paddle with ample cornmeal on it.

With a knuckle punch indentations around the disc. Drizzle olive oil on top. Sprinkle with coarse salt. Carefully slide the focaccia onto the baking stone.

Bake at 400° for 15 to 20 minutes until golden brown and oil is bubbling.

Makes 8 focaccia.

Focaccia Variations

With Onions:
  1 medium onion, thinly sliced

  Place the onion in a small bowl and cover with water. Soak for 10 minutes. Drain and separate into rings. Place the onion on top of the focaccia. Drizzle oil over, sprinkle with salt and proceed with the focaccia recipe.

With Herbs:
  2-4 teaspoons chopped fresh herbs — either rosemary or sage — not both
  30-40 rosemary sprigs or sage leaves

  Add either chopped herb to the dough while kneading. Shape as in focaccia recipe. Drizzle with oil, sprinkle with salt and arrange 4-5 leaves or sprigs of the herbs on top of each focaccia. Proceed with the recipe.

Pizza

½ recipe for Gloria's White Bread, page 183
½ basic tomato sauce, page 45
¼ to ½ pound mozzarella cheese
2-3 Tablespoons olive oil
¼ to ⅓ cup freshly grated Parmesan cheese

Make the bread dough and let it rise until almost doubled. Punch down and shape into balls. Roll out to pizza shape. It can be as thick or thin as you like. You can make 2-3 large pizzas and bake them in pizza pans — or several small ones to bake on a baking stone.

Top with the tomato sauce, sprinkle on the mozzarella, drizzle a little olive oil and top with the grated Parmesan.

Bake at 400° for 15 minutes or until the pizza is browned at the edges and the cheese is golden and bubbly.

You can add any topping you wish before the cheese.

Biscuits

2 cups flour
3 teaspoons baking powder
1 teaspoon salt
1/4 cup shortening, butter, vegetable shortening
                   or vegetable oil
3/4 cup milk

Mix dry ingredients in a mixing bowl. Cut in the shortening with a pastry blender or if using vegetable oil, add it to the milk.

Add the milk or the milk and oil mixture to the flour. Mix quickly. The dough should be soft and puffy but not sticky.

Turn out onto a floured board or counter and knead a few times. Roll or pat out to about 1/2" thick. Do not roll dough too thin. Cut into squares with a knife or cut into rounds with a biscuit cutter.

Place on an ungreased baking sheet. Bake at 400° for 10 to 12 minutes. Serve piping hot! Makes 20 biscuits.

Desserts

DESSERTS

Somehow a meal never seems finished without dessert. It can be as simple as the Tuscan vin santo, a sweet wine, served with biscotti. You dunk the biscotti in the wine, eat the softened biscotti and sip the wine. A lovely way to end a meal.

A dessert can be an elaborate creation. Someone once told me that the secret to a successful dinner party was to serve something wonderful first and a fantastic dessert — as those are what is remembered. And it helps to have interesting people around the table.

Here are a few of my favorite endings. Follow with a cup of espresso or coffee.

Apple Desserts

I absolutely love apple desserts! I spent five days in Paris one fall and had an apple tart for lunch and dinner every day. Each was different and delicious.

My favorite apple dessert is the deep-dish apple pie at the Connaught Hotel in London, although I'm not sure if it's the pie or the Devonshire cream that is poured over it that I like the best.

Here are a few of my favorite apple recipes.

BAKED APPLES

1 apple per person
raisins to fill the center core of each apple
chopped nuts, optional
cinnamon
maple syrup or brown sugar

Core the apples and place in a baking dish.
Fill the center cavity with the raisins. You
can mix in a few chopped nuts if you like.

Sprinkle the tops of the apples with a
bit of cinnamon. Add some maple syrup or
brown sugar if you like. I find the raisins
add enough sweetness — but you may prefer
it a bit sweeter.

Bake at 350° until the apples are tender.
Serve warm — plain or with a little cream
poured on top.

This method works well in the microwave.
Wrap the apples in Saran Wrap. Place in a microwave dish and cook for 5 minutes or until
apples are tender.

Apple Crisp

4 cups apples, pared, cored and sliced — about
               6 medium apples
2/3 – 3/4 cup brown sugar
1/2 cup flour
1/2 cup rolled oats
1/2 teaspoon cinnamon
1/2 teaspoon nutmeg
1/3 cup butter
chopped nuts, optional

      Place sliced apples in a buttered, shallow baking dish — about 1½ quarts in size. The apples should be 1½" to 2" deep.
      Blend the remaining ingredients until the mixture is crumbly. Spread over the apples.
      Bake at 375° until apples are tender and the topping is browned, about 30-35 minutes.
      Serve warm with cream to pour on top, or with ice cream or frozen yogurt.
      Serves 6.

APPLE DUMPLINGS

6 medium apples
pastry for 2 crusts, see page 208
1/2 cup brown sugar
1/4 teaspoon nutmeg
1 teaspoon cinnamon
1/4 cup maple syrup
1/4 cup butter

Peel and core the apples.

Roll out the pastry and cut into 6 squares — the squares need to be large enough to wrap each apple — about 7" square.

Mix the sugar, nutmeg and cinnamon.

Place an apple in the center of each square of pastry. Spoon equal amounts of sugar mixture into each apple cavity. Spoon equal amounts of maple syrup into each cavity. Dot the top of each apple with butter.

Pull the corners of the pastry together, up and around each apple. Pinch the edges together attractively. If you feel really ambitious, you can cut a few leaves out of the pastry and put them on top of each dumpling. Dab a bit of cold water on the edges of the pastry before pinching together —also on the leaves before applying them.

Place in a well-greased baking pan — a 9" x 13" pan should be large enough to hold the dumplings and allow them to brown on all sides.

Bake at 450° for 10 minutes, reduce the heat to 350° and bake until the apples are tender — about 30 to 40 minutes. The crust should be golden brown.

Select a baking pan that has sides, as the apples will give off juices as they bake.

Serve warm with cream or a scoop of ice cream.

Serves 6.

Apple Pie

7-8 cups apples, pared, cored and sliced
3/4 to 1 cup sugar
1 teaspoon cinnamon or
   3/4 teaspoon nutmeg or a combination of both
pastry for 2 crusts, see page 208
1 - 2 Tablespoons butter

   Mix apples, sugar and spices.
   Roll out the bottom crust. Place in a deep
9" pie pate . Pour in apple mixture.
   Roll out top crust. Cut decorative slits
for steam to escape.
   Dot top of apples with butter. Rub the
edge of the pastry with cold water.
   Carefully place top crust on pie. Trim
edges and crimp together decoratively to
seal.
   Bake at 400° for 15 minutes. Reduce heat
to 350° and continue to bake until apples are
bubbling and pastry is golden brown —about
1 hour total baking time.

Deep Dish Apple Pie

8 – 10 cups apples, pared, cored and sliced
juice of 1 lemon
3/4 cup sugar
2 Tablespoons flour
freshly grated nutmeg – about 3/4 teaspoon
pastry for 1 crust, page 208

Combine all ingredients, except pastry, and pour into a deep, flat baking dish. Select a dish so that the apple filling will mound up in the center to create a high rounded crust — about 1½–2 quarts.

Roll out pastry. Cut slits for steam to escape. Place the pastry on top of the apples. Trim the pastry so that it extends evenly all around dish. Fold the edge back onto the top of the pie to create a ½" double crust. Crimp the edge of the pastry.

Bake at 400° for about 1 hour or until apples are tender and bubbling and the pastry is golden brown.

Serve warm with cream or ice cream. Serves 8.

Pie Pastry

enough for a 2 crust 8" to 9" pie
(for one crust pie, halve ingredients)

2 cups flour
1 teaspoon salt
2/3 cup cold lard — butter or a combination of
butter and vegetable shortening may
be used — but I think lard makes the
best pie crust — it should be cold
1/4 cup ice water

In a large bowl mix the flour and the salt.
Add the cold shortening in 2" pieces. Cut it into
the flour with 2 knives or a pastry blender until
the shortening is uniformly mixed with the flour
and the mixture is crumbly. Squeeze a bit of
the mixture together — if it holds together there
is enough shortening — if it crumbles add a
bit more shortening.

Mix in the ice water, a couple of tablespoons at a time, with a fork to incorpor-
ate the water. Add only enough water

to make the dough stick together. With your hands pat the dough together. Do not handle too much.

Shape the dough into 2 flattened discs. Wrap in waxed paper and refrigerate for at least a few hours or overnight.

Roll out the first disc and place in pie plate. Add the filling.

Roll out the second disc. Cut slits in a decorative pattern — to allow steam to escape.

Place on top of filling. Moisten the edges of the bottom pastry by rubbing lightly with cold water. Trim the pastry to the edge of the pie plate. Crimp or pinch the bottom and top edges together to seal them.

My mother always slashed her pie crusts the way her mother did — I still slash mine the same way — a shallow S shape with small slits on each side.

Makes one 2 crust pie or two single crust pies.

Martha's Blue Ribbon
Cherry Pie

4 cups red, tart cherries, pitted
                   you may use canned cherries
1 cup sugar
3 Tablespoons tapioca
1/4 teaspoon almond extract
1 teaspoon lemon juice
1 Tablespoon melted butter
pie pastry for a 2 crust pie, page 208

In a bowl combine all the filling ingredients. If using canned cherries, drain them before adding.

Roll out pastry and line a 9" pie plate. Pour in the filling. Moisten the edge of the pastry with cold water.

Roll out the top crust and make slits for the steam to escape. Place on top of pie, trim edges and crimp crusts together decoratively to seal.

Bake at 425° for 15 minutes. Turn down to 350° and cook until cherries are thick and bubbling and the pastry is golden brown — about 30 minutes.

My sister, Martha, made this pie with a lattice top crust and won a blue ribbon for her pie when she was in high school.

PEACH PIE

4-6 cups fresh, ripe peaches, peeled and
            sliced —about 6-8 peaches
2 Tablespoons lemon juice
1 - 1¼ cups sugar
¼ cup flour
pastry for a 2 crust pie, page 208
a bit of freshly grated nutmeg

Mix the peaches with the lemon juice.
Add the sugar and flour and mix.
    Roll out pastry and line a 9" pie plate.
Pour in the peaches. Grate nutmeg on top.
    Roll out pastry for top crust. Cut
decorative slits for steam to escape. Place
on top of pie. Moisten the bottom crust with
cold water. Crimp edges together.
    Bake at 425° for 15 minutes, turn down
to 375° and cook until peaches are bubbling
and pastry is golden brown — about 45
minutes. Serve slightly warm with ice cream.
    I think peach pie is the very best pie.

Pecan Pie

1/4 cup butter
1 cup brown sugar
3/4 cup light corn syrup
3 eggs, well beaten
1 teaspoon vanilla
2-3 cups pecan halves
brandy or Jack Daniel's, optional
pastry for 1 crust pie, page 208

Melt butter, mix in remaining filling ingredients, reserving 1 cup of the best looking pecan halves for the top. Pour into pie shell. Arrange whole pecan halves on top.

Bake at 350° for 35 to 40 minutes or until custard is firm and pie is golden brown. Serve cool with whipped cream.

I sometimes add a bit of brandy or Jack Daniel's to the custard — about 1/4 cup to 1/3 cup gives a nice touch.

213

Pumpkin Pie

1 1/2 cups canned pumpkin purée
3/4 cup brown sugar
1/2 teaspoon salt
1 teaspoon cinnamon
1/2 teaspoon ginger
1/2 teaspoon nutmeg
1/2 teaspoon cloves
3 eggs, well beaten
1 1/2 cups milk or half-and-half
1/4 cup Bourbon
15-20 whole pecan halves
pastry for 1 crust pie, page 208

To make the filling, in a large bowl mix all the ingredients except the pecans and the pastry.

Roll out the pastry dough and place in a 9" pie plate. On a single crust pie I usually trim the pastry 1/2" to 3/4" larger than the pie plate. Moisten the pastry edge with cold water and fold the extending pastry back toward the pie to create a double pastry edge. Crimp together. This makes a more substantial edge and better-looking pastry.

Pour in the filling. Place a ring of pecan halves around the edge.

Bake at 425° for 15 minutes. Lower the heat to 350° and continue to bake until the custard is set and a knife comes out clean when inserted in the center of the pie — about 40 to 50 minutes.

Serve cooled with whipped cream.

STRAWBERRY SHORTCAKE

216

Strawberry Shortcake

This is one of my favorite spring dishes —
I can make a meal of this.

If you can't use the whole recipe at once,
serve wedges of shortcake, split and topped
with the strawberries. Save the remaining
shortcake for breakfast the next morning. Toast
it and top it with the remaining berries.

1 — 2 quarts fresh, ripe strawberries
sugar to taste
2 cups flour
2 Tablespoons sugar
3 teaspoons baking powder
1 teaspoon salt
1/3 cup vegetable oil
2/3 to 1 cup milk

Clean and hull the strawberries. Sprinkle
sugar to taste on top and set aside while you
make the shortcake. Save a few of the best-
looking berries for garnish — leave the leaves on.

Mix the dry ingredients together in a mixing bowl. Add the oil and 2/3 cup of milk. Mix — if the batter seems dry add a bit more milk. Stir just until blended and spread into a well greased 8" round baking pan.

Bake at 425° for 15 to 20 minutes. Bake until just golden on top and a toothpick comes out clean when inserted in the center.

Invert pan onto a cooling rack and turn out shortcake. With a serrated knife cut the cake into 2 layers.

Crush the strawberries with a fork, enough to create lots of juice but still leave nice pieces of berries.

Place the bottom layer of shortcake on a cake plate and pour half of the strawberries on top. Top with other layer and top that with remaining strawberries. Arrange the reserved berries on top.

Cut and serve immediately.

Pass milk or cream to pour over top.

Serves 6 - 8.

Berry Ice Cream

1 pound fresh, ripe berries — strawberries
            or raspberries
3/4 cup sugar
juice of 1/2 lemon
1/4 cup water
1/2 cup heavy cream

Clean the berries. Put berries, sugar lemon juice and water in a food processor. Purée. If using raspberries, strain the liquid to remove the seeds.

Whip the cream — just to thicken it a bit, not as for whipped cream.

Combine berry mixture and the cream. Taste for sweetness — add more sugar if needed. Chill.

Pour into ice cream freezer and freeze according to manufacturer's instructions. Transfer to a container and store in freezer until ready to serve. Let soften a bit before serving.

Fruit Cobbler

Soft fruits are best for cobblers. Cherries are good. Rhubarb in early spring is tart and delicious — I like to sprinkle brown sugar on rhubarb. Blueberries and peaches are wonderful in summer or try a combination of peaches and blueberries.

3-4 cups ripe, fresh fruit
2/3 to 1 cup sugar
1 cup flour
1 Tablespoon sugar
1 1/2 teaspoons baking powder
1/2 teaspoon salt
3 Tablespoons vegetable oil
1/2 cup milk

Prepare fruit. Mix with sugar to taste in a shallow baking dish — about 1 1/2 quarts. Mix dry ingredients in a bowl. Add the oil and milk and mix only until blended.

Drop batter by spoonfuls onto fruit.

Bake at 400° for 20-30 minutes or until top is golden brown and fruit is tender and bubbling.

Serve warm with milk or cream.

Serves 6-8.

This was one of my father's favorite desserts. Our family made cobbler with the biscuit-type dough as in this recipe, but you can also make a cobbler with pastry dough. Follow the recipe for 1 crust pastry on page 208. Roll into a thin sheet that will cover the fruit. Cut to size of baking dish and place on top of fruit. Bake until fruit is bubbling and thickened and pastry is golden brown.

Pears in Red Wine

4 medium, ripe, firm pears – with
      stems
2-3 cups good red wine
4-6 Tablespoons sugar
4-6 medium bay leaves

   Carefully peel the pears.
Leave the stems on. Remove
the blossom end and pare to
flatten the bottoms so the
pears will stand upright.
   Select a deep saucepan
that will hold the pears
standing up. The pears
should be close
enough to be
held in an

222

upright position — but with enough room so the wine can surround them.

Add enough wine to cover the pears. Add the sugar and the bay leaves.

Cook, covered, over low heat until a toothpick pierces the pears easily. Do not overcook. Transfer the pears to a deep bowl — the pears should stand upright. Add the bay leaves and cover with plastic wrap. Refrigerate overnight or until chilled.

Cook the wine, uncovered, over medium heat until it reduces to a syrup. Chill.

To serve, place each pear in a deep dessert plate or a shallow bowl. Stick a bay leaf into each pear at the stem. Spoon the wine syrup over the pear and bay leaf to glaze them and to make a pool of syrup on the plate.

Select plates that will complement the beautiful burnished red of the pears and the deep red wine sauce.

Serves 4.

My Mother's Rice Pudding

4 Tablespoons rice
4 cups milk
4 Tablespoons sugar
pinch of salt
1/2 teaspoon vanilla or a few grindings
        of fresh nutmeg

Wash the rice in a strainer. Carolina rice is the best rice for puddings. Add all the ingredients to a buttered deep 1 1/2 quart baking dish. Stir.

Bake at 325° for 2 to 3 hours. Stir 2 or 3 times during the first hour. As the pudding cooks it will form a crust on top— let the top get golden brown and the rice thicken to a pudding.

This is an old English recipe from my mother's family. It makes a delicious and unbelievably simple custard. Serve warm.

Serves 4 - 6.

224

Chocolate Mousse

2 squares unsweetened chocolate
1/4 cup chocolate chips
2 egg whites
2 1/2 Tablespoons sugar
1 cup heavy cream, whipped

Melt chocolates over hot but not boiling water in the top of a double boiler. Let cool to lukewarm.

Beat the egg whites until stiff and shiny. Gradually beat in sugar. Fold in whipped cream. Fold in chocolates.

Pour into a 1-pint mold. Chill until firm.

When ready to serve, set mold in warm water for a few seconds to melt and loosen.

Turn onto a serving platter and unmold.

Serve with whipped cream. Or cover the molded mousse with whipped cream and decorate with chocolate shavings.

Never Fail Chocolate Cake

3 cups flour
2 cups sugar
2 teaspoons baking soda
1/2 teaspoon salt
1/4 cup cocoa
1 cup boiling water
2/3 cup vegetable oil
1 cup buttermilk
1 teaspoon vanilla
2 eggs beaten

In a large bowl mix the flour, sugar soda and salt. Mix the cocoa in boiling water until cocoa is dissolved. Add cocoa mixture and remaining ingredients to the flour mixture. Blend well and pour into well greased pans — two 8" round pans or a 9" x 13" oblong one.

Bake at 350° for 20 to 25 minutes for the round cakes or 30 to 35 minutes for the oblong one — or until a toothpick comes out clean after inserting it in the center of the cake.

This easy cake with fudge frosting was a traditional birthday cake. It's been in the family since I was eight or nine. It's the first cake I ever baked and it did fail that first time — because I used baking powder instead of baking soda. It didn't rise and I ended up with what looked like two chocolate rubber discs. Other than that time, I've never known the cake to fail.

The topping for oatmeal cake, page 229 is a delicious option to the fudge frosting.

EASY FUDGE FROSTING

1 cup sugar
1/4 cup butter
1/4 cup cocoa
1/4 cup milk
1 teaspoon vanilla

Mix all the ingredients, except vanilla, in a saucepan. Bring to a boil and boil 1 minute. Remove from heat and add vanilla. Beat until creamy. Spread quickly on cake.

Oatmeal Cake

This is a spicy, moist cake that seems especially good in the fall — we made this cake for my mother's birthday in October. It keeps well.

1 cup oatmeal
1 cup hot water
1/2 cup oil
1 cup sugar
1 cup brown sugar
2 eggs, beaten
1 1/4 cups flour
1 teaspoon salt
1 teaspoon baking soda
1 teaspoon cinnamon

Place oatmeal in a large mixing bowl. Pour hot water over the oatmeal. Add all the remaining ingredients. Mix well.

Pour into well-oiled pans — two 8" round pans or a 9" x 13" oblong one.

Bake at 350° for 20 to 25 minutes for the round pans or 30 to 35 minutes for the oblong one — or until a toothpick comes out clean after inserting it in the center of the cake.

TOPPING FOR OATMEAL CAKE

½ cup milk
½ cup sugar
½ cup butter
1 cup chopped nuts or 1 cup coconut

Mix milk, sugar and butter in a heavy saucepan and cook over medium heat for 5 minutes. Add nuts or coconut or both and mix. Pour over cake while cake is warm.

This topping is also delicious on the never fail chocolate cake on page 226.

MARILYN's CHOCOLATE CHEESECAKE

Crust:
2 Tablespoons softened butter
3 Tablespoons melted butter
3 Tablespoons sugar
1 cup graham cracker crumbs

Spread the soft butter evenly over the sides and bottom of a 9" springform pan.
Combine the melted butter with the sugar and the cracker crumbs. Pat the mixture evenly on the bottom and sides of the pan. Place in the refrigerator while you make the filling.

Filling:
8 ounces semisweet chocolate
1 1/2 pounds mascarpone cheese or other
        mild, soft, creamy cheese
1 cup sugar
2 eggs
1 Tablespoon cocoa

230

1 teaspoon vanilla
1 ½ cups sour cream

Melt the chocolate over hot water. Let cool.

Cream the cheese, sugar and eggs until fluffy. Add the chocolate, cocoa and vanilla and blend. Stir in the sour cream and mix well. Pour into the prepared pan.

Bake at 350° for about 45 minutes. Bake in the middle of the oven, undisturbed.

The cake will shrink slightly from the sides and will be soft in the center. It will firm up later as it chills in the refrigerator.

Open the oven door and let cake cool on the oven rack.

Refrigerate until ready to serve —at least 8 hours.

This is a very rich cake — cut in small pieces it will serve 16.

Instead of graham crackers for the crust, try crumbed chocolate wafers.

BREAKFAST AND BRUNCH

BREAKFAST AND BRUNCH

I love breakfast — especially on a day when I can relax and enjoy a second cup of coffee with _the New York Times_ or with family or friends.

Because we all seem to rush around most mornings, it is a real treat when there is time to prepare and leisurely enjoy a hearty meal — and to linger at the table with a second or third cup of coffee.

Brunch to me is a late breakfast with a Bloody Mary first. Scrambled eggs or a frittata and grilled ham or bacon with muffins or toast are perfect for brunch.

Spiced Stewed Fruit

2 cups assorted dried fruit — any combination
    of prunes, apricots, peaches or pears
1 cinnamon stick
1 - 2 whole cloves
sugar, optional
water to cover

    Put the dried fruit, spices and sugar
in a heavy saucepan. Cover with water. Bring
fruit to a simmer. Cover and simmer until
fruit is plump and tender — about ½ hour.
    Cool fruit. The juices should cover the
fruit — add a bit more water if needed. Cover
with plastic wrap and refrigerate.
    Serve chilled. Serves 4.
    I find the fruit quite sweet without
adding sugar — if you like it sweeter, add
sugar to taste.
    In the winter we often had stewed
prunes as our breakfast fruit — this is more
special with the added spices and mixed fruit.

Jill's Favorite Pancakes

1 cup flour
1 Tablespoon sugar
3 teaspoons baking powder
½ teaspoon salt
2 Tablespoons oil
1 egg
1¼ – 1½ cups milk
butter for greasing griddle
melted butter and warmed maple syrup for
serving with pancakes

Mix dry ingredients in a bowl. Blend oil, egg and milk and pour into dry ingredients. Mix only until all ingredients are blended— the batter should be a bit lumpy.

Heat griddle until water sizzles on it. Brush lightly with butter.

Ladle batter onto hot griddle. Cook until bubbles cover top of pancakes and they are golden brown — this will only take a minute or so. Turn and brown the other side.

I like thin pancakes — so I add milk until the batter is thin, about the consistency of very thick cream. The batter needs to be thick enough to hold a round shape as it is poured onto the hot griddle.

I like to make a big stack of thin pancakes and keep them hot on a warm platter in a warm oven. Serve with melted butter and warm maple syrup.

This is a basic pancake recipe. When my niece, Jill, was visiting me for her tenth-year birthday weekend, I made these pancakes for her. She thought they were the best pancakes she'd ever had!

The secret is to keep them thin!

237

FRENCH TOAST

2- 3 eggs, beaten
1/2 - 3/4 cup milk
pinch of salt
freshly grated nutmeg
8 - 10 slices stale French or Italian bread,
         sliced 1" thick
3-4 Tablespoons butter

    In a flat bowl or deep platter mix eggs with milk. Add salt and nutmeg and mix.

    In a single layer place the bread slices in the egg mixture. Let them soak on one side and turn and soak the other. The bread should be completely saturated with the egg mixture. If necessary, add another egg and more milk. If the bread is stale and dry it could take 1/2 hour for it to be moistened completely.

    On a griddle or in a heavy skillet melt some butter. Add the soaked bread and brown over medium heat.

When the toast is golden brown on one side, flip it over and brown the other side.

The heat should be warm enough to brown the toast but not so hot as to brown it before the egg mixture has cooked and become custard-like in the center. This should take 5-10 minutes over medium heat.

Serve hot with maple syrup or a fruit sauce.

Serves 3-4.

Refrigerator Bran Muffins

2 cups boiling water
2 cups raisins
5 teaspoons baking soda
1 cup vegetable oil
1 cup brown sugar
1 cup light molasses
4 eggs
5 cups flour
1 teaspoon salt
6 cups bran cereal
1 quart buttermilk
1 cup chopped walnuts
½ cup flour

Pour boiling water over raisins and soda. Let cool.

In a large bowl mix oil, brown sugar and molasses. Add the eggs and beat well. Add the flour, salt and cereal to the bowl. Pour in the buttermilk and mix together until blended. Stir in the cooled raisin mixture.

Dredge nuts in ½ cup flour and then fold into batter.

Do not bake when fresh mixed. Store overnight in the refrigerator and bake in the morning.

Fill greased muffin tins ⅔ full and bake at 375° for 25 to 30 minutes.

This batter will keep if covered tightly for a few days in the refrigerator. If you bake all the muffins at once they will freeze well.

These make wonderful giant-sized muffins.

Makes 48 muffins or 20 to 24 giant muffins.

Granola

1 cup honey
1 cup safflower oil or other vegetable oil
5 cups old-fashioned oatmeal
1 cup slivered almonds
1 cup sesame seeds
1 cup sunflower seeds
1 cup shredded coconut
1 cup soy flour
1 cup non-instant powdered milk
1 cup wheat germ

Combine honey and oil. Combine dry ingredients in a large bowl. Add the oil mixture and toss and stir until well mixed. It should be a crumbly mix with nuggets of honey and grains.

Spread on 2 cookie sheets with edges.

Bake at 300° for about 1 hour. Stir every 15 minutes — so it browns evenly. Bake until golden brown.

Cool on cookie sheets. Store in a tightly covered jar or tin or in plastic bags.

This granola is simple to make — all the ingredients are easily found in any heath food store.

It's not too sweet — delicious if you add raisins after it has baked. You can cut back on both the oil and the honey and add some apple juice as part of the liquid.

I've had this recipe since my college days. One of my best friends gave it to me and I always make a batch before traveling. It's great to have a plastic bag full of granola to munch on for breakfast when hotel meals don't seem appealing.

Makes 14 cups of granola.

My Father's Scrambled Eggs

For each serving:
2 eggs
2 Tablespoons milk
1 Tablespoon butter
salt and freshly ground black pepper
additional 1 Tablespoon butter, optional

Break eggs into a bowl add milk and beat until well mixed.

In a heavy skillet melt butter. As soon as butter is melted add the egg mixture. Cook over low heat, stirring and scraping constantly. Slow, even heat makes the best scrambled eggs.

When eggs are beginning to set, season with salt and pepper. I like to add another Tablespoon of butter to give a richer flavor.

Do not overcook. — eggs should be creamy.

Serve immediately with hot buttered toast and crisp bacon.

If you like you can add some chopped fresh herbs with the butter at the end. Chives, chervil and parsley are a good combination with eggs.

You can also add small pieces of smoked salmon and perhaps a bit of chopped dill.

My father always made breakfast for us when we were growing up and this was one of his specialties. It has become one of the main dishes for our traditional "big breakfasts" when all the family has gathered together.

FRITTATA

246

FRITTATA

Frittata is the Italian version of an omelet. It is cooked over low heat and is cooked on both sides. It is a wonderfully easy dish — and can be made with eggs or with eggs and any sort of cooked vegetable.

6 eggs, beaten
1/2 — 3/4 cup freshly grated Parmesan cheese
2-3 Tablespoons butter

Mix the Parmesan cheese with the eggs. Melt butter in a medium heavy skillet over medium heat. Pour in eggs, stir and cook for a few minutes until the eggs begin to thicken. Continue to cook until eggs are set and firm. Loosen the frittata.
Put a large plate over the skillet and turn the skillet and plate over. The frittata should be on the plate. Slide it back into the skillet and cook the other side.

The frittata should not brown — it should be golden and the eggs just cooked through.

Slide onto a serving platter. Cut into wedges and serve.

If you prefer, instead of inverting the frittata, you can put the skillet under a hot broiler to set the top of the eggs. Loosen the frittata and slide it onto a serving platter.

This is a good lunch or brunch dish — or a quick and easy supper. It will pack well and is good for a picnic meal eaten at room temperature.

I have not added salt as I find the Parmesan cheese is salty enough. If you prefer the frittata a bit saltier — add salt.

Serves 2-3.

FRITTATA VARIATIONS

Frittata with mozzarella and herbs:

1/2 cup diced mozzarella
1/4 cup chopped fresh herbs
1 recipe for frittata, page 247

Proceed with basic recipe. When eggs are just beginning to set stir in mozzarella and herbs. I particularly like parsley, chives and chervil or parsley, chives and basil. You may use any combination you like.

Frittata with onions:

3-4 medium onions, sliced
2-3 Tablespoons olive oil
1 recipe for frittata, page 247

Sauté the onions in the oil in a heavy skillet over low heat. The onions should cook slowly and gradually brown.

249

When onions have browned proceed with the basic frittata recipe. Add the onions to the egg mixture when it is beginning to set. Finish as in the basic recipe.

Frittata with vegetables:

1 - 1½ cups cooked vegetables
1 recipe for frittata, page 247

Use the recipe on page 126 for mushrooms with garlic, or page 131 for zucchini with garlic, or page 128 for eggplant with onions. All are excellent added to the basic frittata recipe.

Cook the vegetables as each recipe indicates. Proceed with the basic frittata recipe. Add the vegetables just as the eggs begin to set. Continue as for the basic frittata.

Frittata with potatoes and onions:

2-3 Tablespoons olive oil
1 medium onion, thinly sliced
2-3 medium potatoes, thinly sliced
Salt and freshly ground black pepper
1 recipe for basic frittata, page 247

Pour the oil into a medium-sized heavy skillet. Add the onions and cook over medium heat until they begin to wilt. Add potatoes and cook until the potatoes are tender and browned. This will take about 20 to 25 minutes. Watch the heat so the onions don't get too brown.

Make the basic frittata recipe and add the potatoes and onions along with the eggs. Continue to cook as the recipe indicates.

This is a terrific lunch or late supper along with a green salad and a glass of wine.

Picnics

PICNICS

    I love eating "al fresco" — outdoors. Even a sunny winter day in the woods is fun — if you can find a windfree spot along a trail for a quick cup of hot soup and a sandwich.

    I have many memories of picnics when we were children. We would carry our simple lunch out to the old cherry tree in the yard and sit on the grass to eat our sandwiches. One of my favorites was a sandwich made with tomatoes that we had just picked in the garden and that were still warm from the sun. The tomatoes were cut into thick slices and placed on thick slices of homemade bread that had been generously spread with mayonnaise. I still love this simple and delicious sandwich.

    I remember beautiful fall days and hikes through the woods at Allardale, the farm where my father grew up and which my uncle Stanley has lovingly made more beautiful each year.

My father liked to check out the squirrels and their nests before hunting season. We would gather acorns and hickory nuts. If it was warm we would wade in the creek.

We would cook breakfast over a wood fire. There is still nothing like the smells of breakfast cooking over a wood fire—especially on a crisp fall morning.

There were also the big elaborate picnics, church or family gatherings and the typical All-American Fourth of July picnic.

My father's idea of a good picnic was potato salad, page 257, baked beans, page 156, and a baked ham, page 258. Bread and butter pickles and my mother's bran rolls were the finishing touches.

Dessert was a freshly baked fruit pie or Grandma Allard's ice cream.

A picnic does not have to be elaborate—

it can be as simple as an early morning cup of coffee with a piece of toast and jam on the terrace while watching the mist rise over the hills.

Or it can be a basket filled with bread, salami, cheese, fruit and a sweet. Add a bottle of wine and some water.

It can be a very elaborate affair — baskets carefully packed with your best pottery and glasses along with a linen tablecloth and napkins, and a blanket— perhaps for a concert in the park.

However you do it, dining "al fresco" is a treat.

Potato Salad with Dill

8-10 small new potatoes
salt
1/2 cup sour cream or yogurt
1/4 cup mayonnaise
1/2 cup onion, finely chopped
1 cucumber, peeled, seeded, sliced, salted
                        and drained
1/3 cup chopped dill

Scrub potatoes. Place in a pot with salted water to cover. Cover and cook until tender but firm — about 10 to 15 minutes. Do not overcook. Drain, cut into quarters or halves.

Add sour cream or yogurt and mayonnaise, which have been mixed together. Toss gently. Add cucumbers, onions and dill and toss again. Taste for salt. Cool and refrigerate.

Before serving toss again. Correct seasonings. Add more sour cream or yogurt if salad seems dry. Serves 4-6.

Ham Baked with Mustard, Brown Sugar and Cider

1 ham, ready to bake (allow 1/2 pound per serving)
2-3 cups cider
3/4 cup brown sugar
1-2 teaspoons dry mustard
whole cloves

If you are using an uncooked ham allow 1/2 hour cooking time per pound. If you are using a fully cooked ham allow 10 minutes per pound to heat through.

Place ham in a heavy roasting pan. Pour cider in pan to 1/2" depth. Bake at 325°. Baste ham frequently with cider. Add more cider if it begins to evaporate. The ham will give off some juices, add more liquid only to keep juices from scorching.

One hour before estimated finished cooking time — remove ham from oven.

If there is skin on the ham peel it off with a knife. With the knife score the ham

258

on the diagonal and then score again across the original score marks to make a diamond grid. Stick a clove into the center of each diamond.

Make a glaze of the brown sugar, mustard and enough cider to make a paste. Cover the ham with the glaze.

Return ham to oven and continue to bake and baste with cider. If you are using an uncooked ham, it should read 160° to 170° on a meat thermometer for the ham to be completely cooked. A precooked ham needs to heat through — to 130° to 135° on the thermometer.

Serve the ham hot, room temperature or cooled.

GRANDMA ALLARD'S
ICE CREAM

260

Grandma Allard's Ice Cream

3 quarts milk
2½ cups sugar
1 cup flour
1 teaspoon salt
7-8 eggs, beaten
1 pint cream or half-and-half
5 teaspoons vanilla

In a large, heavy saucepan heat 2 quarts milk over medium heat. In a bowl mix the sugar, flour and salt. Add the remaining quart of milk and stir to mix. Add the cold milk mixture to the hot milk stirring constantly. Turn the heat to medium low and cook until until the custard has thickened, stirring constantly.

Remove from heat. Add a little of the hot custard to the eggs to warm them. Stir and slowly add eggs to the custard, stirring constantly, until it is all incorporated.

Cook over very low heat for a few minutes. Pour into a 6-quart ice cream freezer. Cool — at least to room temperature — or chill. The ice cream will freeze faster if it is chilled.

When ready to freeze add the cream or half-and-half to the custard. Add milk until the freezer is 3/4 full. You may add part half-and-half if you like your ice cream richer.

Add vanilla.

Freeze according to the manufacturer's instructions until the freezer stops and the custard has become ice cream.

There is nothing quite like homemade ice cream. When I was a child we would make ice cream for summer picnics, and all of the children got to turn the crank on the freezer. Anyone who helped churn the ice cream could lick the freezer paddle.

Now that ice cream freezers are electrified, some of the mystique is gone — but not the flavor!

CHRISTMAS FOODS

CHRISTMAS

    I love everything about Christmas. It is a wonderful time of year. The spirit of Christmas seems to fill everyone with joy and good cheer.

    I love the giving of gifts — all the planing, shopping and wrapping gives me great pleasure.

    I love the sound of Christmas carols and the smell of Christmas — the fresh piney aroma of the tree and the wonderful kitchen smells of baking bread and gingery cookies.

    I love the tradition of food and family and being together.

    Over the years our holiday meals have settled into a tradition. Because the day before Christmas is so busy with family arriving and last minute errands, supper on Christmas Eve is a simple meal of a hearty soup, a big green salad and crusty homemade bread. Dessert is a big compote of fruit and a grand tray of Christmas cookies.

Breakfast on Christmas morning is one of our traditional "big breakfasts" with the addition of pecan butterscotch rolls and the festive orange wreath rolls along with an orange from our stocking.

Our Christmas dinner has rarely varied over the years. The center is the golden brown turkey and lots of dressing. It is accompanied by mashed potatoes, page 144, puréed butternut squash, page 135, perhaps a green vegetable like peas or broccoli or possibly mashed turnips. Glazed parsnips are also a possibility. Cranberry relish, page 273, homemade pickles and my mother's bran rolls, page 189, complete the meal. Aunt Esther will bring a fabulous dessert— probably one of her special pies.

We all eat too much and linger over coffee and share remembrances of Christmases past.

Roast Turkey with Dressing

1 large fresh turkey – about 20 - 22 pounds
salt and freshly ground black pepper
1/3 cup softened butter
1 - 2 Tablespoons chopped rosemary

Rinse the turkey well in a few changes of water. Reserve the neck and giblets.

Pat the turkey dry inside and out with paper towels. Salt and pepper the inside cavity and stuff with dressing, page 268.

Skewer the opening and truss and tie it closed. Salt and pepper the neck cavity and stuff it with the dressing. Skewer the opening and lace it and tie it closed. Do not pack the dressing in as it will expand as it cooks.

Tie the wings and legs to the body of the turkey.

Rub butter on the outside of the turkey. Pat salt, pepper and rosemary on the turkey.

Place the turkey on a rack in a large roasting pan.

Roast at 325°, basting the turkey with the pan juices every 20-30 minutes. You can use a little broth to baste until the juices are ready. Roast until the turkey is tender and its joints move easily, about 15-20 minutes per pound.

Remove the turkey to a large carving board and let it rest 15 minutes before carving.

In the Allard family making the turkey and the dressing is a community affair. On Christmas eve a group gathers around the table and breaks bread. Our family loves dressing — so we always make a lot. We mix it in a large metal antique pan.

DRESSING FOR TURKEY

3-5 medium to large loaves homemade bread—
    we use a combination of white and whole
    wheat — whatever we have that is a bit
    stale
3-4 medium onions, chopped
12-15 stalks celery, chopped — add a few
    chopped leaves
several sprigs parsley, chopped
1 cup butter
3-4 Tablespoons sage, or to taste
3-4 teaspoons rosemary, or to taste
3-4 teaspoons thyme, or to taste
salt and freshly ground black pepper
6-8 eggs, beaten

    Tear the bread into ½" pieces. If the
bread is fresh, tear it into pieces and let
it dry out for a day.
    In a large, heavy skillet melt the
butter. Add the onion and cook until
it has softened. Add the celery and cook

until it has softened, about 5 more minutes. Add the parsley.

Pour the vegetables over the bread. Mix until the vegetables are evenly distributed.

Add the herbs and salt and pepper to taste. If using fresh herbs chop the sage, rosemary and thyme together. If using dry herbs the sage and thyme leaves will crumble easily, but the rosemary needles need to be chopped. You will need less of the dried herbs.

The challenging part is mixing and tasting, and seasoning and mixing yet again until all in the family agree that there is exactly enough salt, and precisely enough sage and just the right amounts of rosemary and thyme.

Keep the dressing in a cool place until you are ready to stuff the turkey.

When ready to use, add the eggs and mix well. With so much dressing there is enough to fill one or two casserole dishes as well as stuff the turkey.

Butter the casserole dishes and fill with the dressing. Pour a little broth on top, cover and bake for 30-40 minutes. Uncover and continue to bake and to brown the top for 15 minutes more.

GIBLET BROTH

neck and giblets from 1 turkey
1 medium onion, quartered
1 stalk celery, cut in 2" pieces, plus a
       few celery leaves
2-3 sprigs parsley
1/4 teaspoon thyme leaves
salt and a few peppercorns

Place giblets in a saucepan. Add the vegetables and the seasonings. Cover with water. Bring to a simmer and cook for 45 minutes to 1 hour. Discard the vegetables and the neck. Reserve the giblets. Strain the broth. Makes about 1 quart.

To Make the Gravy

Pour the pan juices from the roasting pan into a large, heavy pan. Scrape all the browned bits into the pan juices. If there is a lot of fat skim some of it off, but leave enough to give body and flavor to the gravy. Add the giblet broth, page 270.

Make a thickening of 2 cups water and 1 cup flour. Whisk or beat well — make sure there are no lumps.

Add milk to the pan juices. Taste as you add the milk — do not dilute the flavor of the gravy. You should have about 8 cups liquid. Bring it to a boil. Slowly add the thickening, stirring constantly. Add only enough to thicken the gravy — you may not need it all. Let the gravy come to a boil and turn down heat and let the gravy simmer for 10 minutes. Taste for seasonings. You will need to add salt.

You may add the reserved giblets — which have been chopped. In our house we add giblets to some of the gravy and leave some plain.

271

CRANBERRY RELISH

CRANBERRY RELISH

4 cups cranberries
1-2 oranges, cut in quarters, seeds removed but with peels
1-2 cups sugar

Put cranberries and orange wedges in a food processor. Chop coarsely — do not chop to fine — you want to have bits of the fruit for texture.

Pour into a bowl and mix in sugar. I like this a bit tart, so I start with a generous cup of sugar. Let stand to mellow overnight.

Taste and add more sugar if needed. Serve in a pretty crystal bowl. This is a lovely relish for turkey or ham. It keeps well in the refrigerator.

Gingerbread Boys and Girls

⅓ cup softened butter
1 cup light brown sugar
1½ cups dark molasses
⅔ cup cold water

274

6 cups flour
2 teaspoons baking soda
1 teaspoon salt
1 teaspoon ginger
1 teaspoon cinnamon
1 teaspoon cloves
1 teaspoon allspice

In a large bowl mix butter, sugar and molasses. Stir in water. Mix the dry ingredients together and stir into the sugar mixture. Blend together. Pat the dough into 2 flattened discs. Wrap in waxed paper and chill for 3 to 4 hours or overnight. This is a very soft dough and must be cold to roll out easily.

Roll out one of the discs on a lightly floured board to about 1/4" to 1/3" thick. Do not roll too thin. These cookies are better thick and chewy. Cut into gingerbread boys and girls with cookie cutters. Reindeer and teddy bears are also good.

Select cookie cutters that are simple shapes and are not intricate, as the dough will stick in small openings.

Place cookies on a well-greased cookie sheet — leave enough room for the cookies to expand.

Bake at 350° for 8 to 12 minutes — or until no imprint remains when touched. Do not overbake.

These are traditional Christmas cookies and we decorate them with a powdered sugar icing, recipe on following page, that has been colored and thinned slightly so it will flow easily from a decorating tube or a small plastic bag with a tiny hole cut in one corner. The icing may be squeezed out to create hair, eyes, noses, mouths and decorative buttons, bows, etc.

Great fun for children of all ages!

Decorating Icing

3 cups powdered sugar
1/4 cup softened butter
2-3 Tablespoons cream
1/2 teaspoon vanilla
food coloring
1 egg white, optional

Blend sifted powdered sugar with butter and cream. Add more sugar or more cream to desired consistency. Make it thicker and creamier if spreading on cookies. Add more liquid if using a pastry tube or plastic bag.

Add vanilla and beat well. Divide icing into small bowls — one for each color desired. Mix in food coloring slowly until the color suits you.

Decorate cookies. Let cookies dry for a few hours so icing will set.

You can use eggwhites for part of the cream — eggwhites will make a harder glaze.

GRANDMA INDOE'S BROWN SUGAR COOKIES

5 cups flour
1 teaspoon baking powder
1 teaspoon baking soda
1 teaspoon salt
2 cups brown sugar
1 cup butter, vegetable shortening or lard
3 Tablespoons cold water
3 eggs, beaten
1 teaspoon vanilla

Mix dry ingredients in a large mixing bowl. If you are using butter or lard, cut it in with 2 knives or a pastry blender as if making pastry. Grandma always used lard. I use butter and my sister, Marianne, uses vegetable oil. Butter gives a real buttery taste — vegetable oil makes a moist and chewy cookie.

If using vegetable oil, mix it in with the water, eggs and vanilla.

Add the liquid to dry ingredients. Shape into 3 flattened discs and wrap in waxed paper. Chill for 3 to 4 hours or overnight.

Roll each disc out on a lightly floured board and cut into desired shapes. Place on a well-greased cookie sheet.

Bake at 375° for about 8 minutes — until no depression remains when touched lightly with a finger.

Cool on cooling rack.

When we were young and visited Grandma Indoe, she had a big jar of these sugar cookies as a treat for us. She cut these cookies into a scalloped round shape and sprinkled them with sugar before baking.

I use this recipe for Christmas cookies — cut into Christmasy shapes and decorated with icing.

Marianne's Chocolate Chip Cookies

2¼ cups flour
1 teaspoon baking soda
1 teaspoon salt
¾ cup brown sugar
¾ cup sugar
1 cup vegetable oil
2 eggs
1 teaspoon vanilla
1 12 ounce package
   or 2 cups chocolate
   chips

Mix dry ingredients in a large mixing bowl. Add oil, eggs and vanilla and mix well. Add chocolate chips and stir in.

Drop the cookie dough from a teaspoon onto an ungreased baking sheet.

Bake at 350° for about 10 – 12 minutes. Do not overbake. Keep them soft and chewy.

Cool on a cooling rack.

Store in a closed container — these do not stay around for long — the most popular cookie in our family.

Marianne adds ½ cup oatmeal with the dry ingredients when she wants a thicker, chewier cookie. The oatmeal also adds vitamins, minerals and fiber to the cookies.

You may also add ½ cup chopped nuts to either version.

FRUIT AND NUT DROPS

3 cups seedless raisins
1/2 cup Bourbon
1 1/2 cups flour
1 1/2 teaspoons baking soda
1 1/2 teaspoons cinnamon
1/2 teaspoon each nutmeg and cloves
1/4 cup softened butter
1/2 cup packed brown sugar
2 eggs
1 pound pecan halves
1/4 pound diced citron
1 pound whole candied red cherries
        or 1/2 pound each red and green

Put raisins in a small bowl. Pour Bourbon over and stir. Let stand 1 hour.
Mix dry ingredients.
In a large bowl beat the butter and sugar. Add the eggs and beat well.
Beat in flour mixture. Stir in raisins

and Bourbon. Add the pecans, citron and cherries. Mix well.

Drop from a teaspoon onto a well-greased baking sheet.

Bake at 325° for about 15 minutes—or until firm.

Cool on cooling rack.

Store in an airtight tin.

These are a nice alternative to fruitcake — if you don't want to go into the big production of making fruitcake. These are quick and easy and they keep well.

MARIANNE'S BROWNIES

²/3 cup cocoa
3/4 cup vegetable oil
2 cups sugar
4 eggs
1 teaspoon vanilla
1 1/4 cups flour
1 teaspoon baking powder
1 teaspoon salt
1 cup chopped walnuts

Mix cocoa and oil together. Add sugar, eggs and vanilla and beat until well blended. Stir in the dry ingredients. Add the nuts and mix.

Pour into a well-greased 9" x 13" baking pan.

Bake at 350° for 25 to 30 minutes. Do not overbake. Cook until brownies begin to pull away from the edges of the pan and the center leaves a very slight impression when lightly touched.

Cool on cooling rack. Cut into squares when brownies are still slightly warm. Cool and remove them from pan. Store in an airtight container.

Pecan Butterscotch Rolls

½ recipe sweet roll dough, page 192
¼ cup softened butter
½ cup sugar
1 – 1½ teaspoons cinnamon
2 – 3 cups pecans, halves or pieces
½ cup butter
⅔ cup brown sugar
2 Tablespoons light corn syrup

Prepare dough and let rise until doubled.
Roll out dough into an oblong shape—
about 9" x 15" and ½" thick.
Spread dough with softened butter.
Mix sugar and cinnamon and sprinkle over
butter. Sprinkle about 1 cup pecans on top.
Roll up tightly as for jelly roll to create
a long loglike roll. Cut into 1¼" thick slices.
To make butterscotch:
Melt butter, mix in brown sugar and
corn syrup.
Cover the bottom of a 9" x 13" baking pan

with butterscotch mixture. Sprinkle pecans — enough to generously cover bottom of pan.

Place sliced rolls, spiral side facing up, on top of pecans. Let rise until doubled.

Bake at 375° for 25 to 30 minutes.

Remove from oven and immediately turn pan upside down on a large sheet of aluminum foil that has been placed on a cooling rack. Let pan remain for a few minutes to let all the butterscotch run down onto the rolls. Serve warm.

If you make the rolls in advance wrap them in aluminum foil until ready to serve. Open ends of foil to let steam escape and reheat at 325° for 20 to 25 minutes — until heated through.

These rolls may be made into individual "sticky buns." Pour butterscotch mixture into well-greased extra-large muffin cups. Place slice of dough into each cup and let double. Bake at 375° for 15-20 minutes. Turn pan upside down to let butterscotch cover buns.

ORANGE WREATH ROLLS

288

Orange Wreath Rolls

½ recipe sweet roll dough, page 192
3 Tablespoons softened butter
¼ to ½ cup brown sugar
grated rind of 1 lemon and 2 oranges
Icing:
    3 Tablespoons softened butter
    1 Tablespoon each grated lemon and
           orange rind
  juice of 1 orange
  1 – 1½ cups powdered sugar

Prepare dough and let rise until doubled.
Roll out dough into an oblong about
9" x 18" and ½" thick. Spread softened
butter on dough. Sprinkle brown sugar to
cover. Add grated rinds, sprinkling evenly
over dough. Roll up as for jelly roll into
a long loglike roll.
Place on a well-greased baking
sheet, sealed edge down. Bring the two
ends together to make a ring. With

clean kitchen scissors, make perpendicular cuts 2/3 of the way into the ring at 1" intervals.

Turn each 1" section on its side so that the spiral shows. Spread and flatten each — arranging all the spiral dough sections so you have a fluted or scalloped ring that is higher in the center where the spirals are connected and flattened at the outside fluted edge of the ring.

Let rise until almost doubled.

Bake at 375° for 25 to 30 minutes.

Make orange icing by combining butter, lemon and orange rinds and orange juice. Add powdered sugar and mix to make a creamy icing. Add more powdered sugar if necessary.

Spread the icing on the warm rolls, let it drizzle into the rolls and down the sides. I carefully tie a big red ribbon around the rolls to make the ring of rolls look like a Christmas wreath. Serve warm.

If you make the rolls ahead, reheat as in previous recipe. Add the icing and ribbon.

INDEX

ABOUT THE AUTHOR

Linda Allard, design director for Ellen Tracy, grew up in a family that was always interested in creative endeavors — including the making of good food. From a young age she knew that she wanted to become involved in fashion design, and by the age of ten she was sewing and designing her own clothes. Today, as the creative force of the Ellen Tracy fashion group, she is one of Seventh Avenue's most respected leaders.

In addition to her fast-paced work life, Linda always makes time to relax in her country home and to enjoy her related hobbies of cooking and gardening. Her interest in combining these two pastimes led her to create this cookbook, which was originally done as a handmade Christmas present for family and friends. Now, with the publication of <u>Absolutely Delicious</u>, she hopes to bring her simple but inventive recipes to a much wider audience.